MARRIAGE
GOD'S WAY

MARRIAGE
GOD'S WAY

HENRY BRANDT & KERRY L. SKINNER

BROADMAN
&HOLMAN
PUBLISHERS

Nashville, Tennessee

0-8054-1971-3

Published by Broadman & Holman Publishers, Nashville, Tennessee
Editorial Team: Leonard G. Goss, John Landers, Sandra Bryer
Page Design and Typesetting: PerfecType, Nashville, TN

Dewey Decimal Classification: 248
Subject Heading: MARRIAGE

Library of Congress Cataloging-in-Publication Data

Brandt, Henry R.
    Marriage God's way / by Henry Brandt and Kerry L. Skinner.
        p. cm.
    ISBN 0-8054-1971-3 (hardcover)
    1. Marriage—Religious aspects—Christianity. 2. Marriage—Biblical teaching.
I. Skinner, Kerry L., 1955–   . II. Title.
    BV4596.M3B69   1999
248.4—dc21
                                                                99-23279
                                                                    CIP

1 2 3 4 5 03 02 01 00 99

Dedication

To the multitude of couples who have asked for help toward a biblical solution to their marital problems. Together we have seen Bible-based solutions evaporate interpersonal problems. That gives me confidence to write this book.

To Jo, my loving wife, who helps me remain faithful to the writing task by taking care of an enormous load of details.

Acknowledgments

Without Kerry Skinner's timeless and efficient help, there would be no book. We took the principles from *I Want My Marriage to Be Better* (1976, now out of print) and added new insights gained since that book was written. This book is the result. I have witnessed Kerry and his wife Elaine practice many of these principles in their own marriage.

Steve and Julie Thomas gave invaluable help in improving and clarifying our writing style. I have observed them as they applied some of these principles to enrich their marriage and also in giving counsel to a steady stream of couples who turn to them for help.

And to Mike and Deborah Shepherd, who make it their aim to use biblical guidelines in their family life and in their ministry. I salute them as I observe the result.

Contents

Marriage God's Way

By Henry T. Blackaby

R ight now in your life, you are right in the middle of some of the deepest movings of God that you will ever know. You are not in isolation. The God we serve is a God of history. God is pursuing you and your family just as clearly as He was pursuing Abraham.

Many times people in the Bible are seen as heroes. God purposed that we should remember them. Abraham had no idea that God would use his act of faith as an example to all future generations. His life would become the pacesetter for faith in the lives of all the children of God.

Peter, the fisherman, had no idea when Jesus called him that everybody until the end of time would talk about his life. But the God who met Abraham and Peter in the simple moments of life is exactly the same God who is wanting to impact your marriage.

God is just as personal—just as present—just as real—today! He knows what He has in mind for your life and your family. God gave these and other examples in Scripture so we could know Him and His ways. That is why Henry Brandt and Kerry Skinner have titled this book *Marriage God's Way*. They wanted you to know God's ways as they pertain to marriage.

The only reason God put the Scripture together is so that we could know what He is up to, so that when God is moving in your life you will know it is God. You must learn to make the connection between what God did in history and what He is doing in your life today. Then you can look at what is happening and say, "That's something that only God can do." The Scripture must be the central point in learning God's way for marriage.

For instance, unless God enabled you to do His will, you'd never even want to do His will. The Scripture states

> **As it is written:**
> *"There is none righteous, no, not one;*
> *There is none who understands*
> *There is none who seeks after God."*
> ROMANS 3:10–11

Because of sin, none seek after God. Who is included in none? Everybody. Does that include you? God also says,

> **For it is God who works in you both to will and**
> **to do for *His* good pleasure.**
> PHILIPPIANS 2:13

God is at work causing you to want to do His will—and then enabling you to do it. God will help you to clarify that there is something happening on the inside of you that only God could do. But when you come to the place from the Scripture where you understand that what is happening in your marriage and in your home, or in your life personally, is something that only God can do, it puts a whole different light on everything.

Right now God is mightily at work around you—in your marriage and in your home and in your life. There are a couple of Scriptures that God can use to bring to your remembrance some things about what He is doing in your life.

The first one is John 13:20.

> **"Most assuredly, I say to you, he who receives**
> **whomever I send receives Me; and he who receives**
> **Me receives Him who sent Me."**
> JOHN 13:20

In this chapter Jesus took a towel and girded Himself and washed the disciples' feet. Then He turned to them and told them that whatever they saw Him do, they should do to one another.

> **"For I have given you an example, that you should**
> **do as I have done to you."**
> JOHN 13:15

Why did Jesus wash their feet? Because they were dirty and nobody else had done it, and because these were His friends and He loved them. So He simply did the most loving thing that a friend would do. Then He told them they should do as He had done.

Does that apply to your marriage? Yes! As a matter of fact, preeminently it applies to your marriage. It does not mean that every night you wash each other's feet. It does mean if anything would be an expression of love towards your partner, you ought not to wait for someone else to do it—you ought to take the initiative. Love always takes the initiative. Love always seeks an opportunity to serve.

Jesus taught that whoever receives the one God sends receives Christ. Let me put that in very careful language and then apply it to your marriage and life. Jesus was teaching His disciples that long before they ever recognized the activity of God, He was at work around them. God will send people to you, and you will see people come to your life. People coming into your life is not just a wonderful coincidence. God deliberately sends people to you. God sent your marriage partner to you.

God was working in my wife Marilynn's life twenty-one years before I ever met her. By the time God brought her to me, she was the sum total of the love of God having worked for twenty-one years to shape her to be the person that she had become. Jesus helped me to understand that He had sent Marilynn to me. I understood that God sent her to me, and how I received her, I would receive Christ—and how I receive Christ, I receive the Father who sent Him. That is awesome, isn't it?

God sent you your marriage partner. However you treat her or him, however you respond, you are responding directly to Christ and His Father. Why is it so crucial for husbands to understand this?

> **Likewise, you husbands, dwell with *them* with understanding, giving honor to the wife, as to the weaker vessel, and as *being* heirs together of the grace of life, that your prayers may not be hindered.**
> 1 PETER 3:7

Men, be very careful how you treat your wives. You need to treat them with honor as joint heirs, because if you do not treat them rightly it will hinder your prayers. Your prayer life is dramatically affected by the way you treat your wife. How you receive and treat the one God sent you is how you treat Him. Can you imagine mistreating your wife and then asking God to bless you? God would say, "Do you know what you just did to Me?" You might think, *Lord, it wasn't unto You; it was my wife, and you don't know my wife.* But God does know your wife—in fact, better than you do.

When God brought your marriage partner, He knew exactly what He was doing. God created us interdependent; we need one another. God matched you with someone He worked on for years. That's why, by the way, when Marilynn and I were courting, I said to her, "I want you to tell me every vow you made to God because I want to spend the rest of our lives helping you fulfill them."

Vows made to God are made in tender moments of your relationship to Him. You do not cancel all the vows you made to God because you married someone. As a matter of fact, all the vows you made to God need to be known by your partner if the partner is to help you fulfill them. This prepares the way for God to bless your home. When you respond to your spouse, you respond to Him who made an investment in his or her life and who indwells that life.

Someone has said that whenever God had a mighty deed to be accomplished, He caused a child to be born. When God wanted to deliver the children of Israel out of bondage, He caused Moses to be born. When God was looking for a mighty leader, He caused Samuel to be born. When God wanted a forerunner to prepare the way for the Son of God, He caused John the Baptist to be born. When He wanted someone to begin a whole nation, He caused Isaac to be born.

If you have children, how have you treated the children when they were born or adopted into your home? How we treat children, we treat Him. When things get rough and they go through their teen years, do you still remember that they were brought to you by God? Do you understand that those children were His before they were yours? And He gave them to you, for He had something in mind for them. How you treat your children, you treat Christ and you treat the Father.

I've talked to many parents who've said, "You know, I think that God was talking to my child, but I was so busy and caught up with other things that I said, 'Well later, later'—but there never was a later." The child may never come back to talk again. But in that moment, God was at work in your child. Remember, how you respond to the one He sends you, you respond to Him. Realize that if you put off your child, you put off the Lord who had suddenly let you know that something very significant was happening.

Do you want to experience marriage God's way? If so, remember the great love of God that sent your marriage partner. As you read this book, take time to meditate on the Scriptures. When you come across a Scripture, stop and look it up in your Bible. Highlight the verse and make any notes about how God impacts you with the verse. Remember, God's ways are not our ways. Look to Him for "the way, the truth, and the life" as it pertains to your relationship with your spouse.

Henry T. Blackaby

CHAPTER 1

Building a Solid Foundation

Let nothing be *done* through selfish ambition or conceit, but in lowliness of mind let each esteem others better than himself.

PHILIPPIANS 2:3

"**I** want to be a better partner." You say this, thinking back over a multitude of incidents that make up the history of your family. Some of them were funny when they happened; others are funny only as we look back on them. Still others were gravely serious. Some were puzzling.

There are months on end when husband and wife get along beautifully; and then, out of the clear blue sky, there are frequent disagreements. Then, just as mysteriously, things clear up.

This is the ebb and flow, the fascination, the never-ending variety, the multitude of moods that make up family living. How can we do our part better?

Seldom, if ever, do the circumstances of living together transform the two people of a marriage into an ever-loving, ever-agreeable, happy pair—fairy tales, popular love songs, and a gamble of fate notwithstanding.

A happy marriage involves a much greater challenge than simply finding a partner with whom you live happily ever after. It is more than some strange chemistry that draws and holds you together forever. Soon after the wedding day you realize that marriage is a test of your character.

A happy marriage does not depend on perfectly matched partners. It is a lifetime process dependent on many choices made by two free individuals who deliberately choose the same harness and who continuously sacrifice personal freedom and self-interest for a mutually agreeable way of life.

Everyone has at least a few good points—ability, talent, a unique kind of charm, interesting mannerisms, or pleasing ways.

Put two people together, and before long irritations, conflicts, or differences of opinion arise in spite of the assets.

BEFORE THE WEDDING

Nancy was an office manager with a dozen people reporting to her. At church, she was an efficient, dependable Sunday school secretary.

With a few girlfriends she played tennis, watched the major league baseball games, and went to local basketball and football games. Work, church, and sports kept her pleasantly occupied. But Nancy was pushing thirty.

"How come I'm not married?" It was a question she asked more and more as she looked in the mirror at her pretty face and her trim, shapely figure.

Then along came Ken. He showed up at church—an easygoing extrovert with a friendly grin, an easy manner, a white BMW, and a pocket full of money. He liked sports too. But at the ball park, instead of getting bleacher seats, where Nancy chose to sit, Ken got box seats. They went to the best restaurants, and he bought her nice gifts and sent flowers. Nancy battled him tenaciously on the tennis court. She loved to listen to him chatter, and he enjoyed being listened to. Their courtship was pleasant and happy, but there were also some questions.

She thought Ken was too extravagant with money. Maybe he talked too much and dressed too casually. But he was responsible, had a good job, and could afford to be lavish with his money.

He thought Nancy was too quiet and conservative, but he felt he needed someone like her.

AFTER THE WEDDING

So they got married, with all the money they needed, and drove a BMW on their honeymoon to Florida.

Although the whirlwind courtship had lasted seven months, Nancy still was not used to a big car or fast driving. She was used to driving at speeds around 55 to 60 miles an hour. But in his big, powerful BMW, Ken took off at 80 miles an hour the moment they got on the freeway. The speed bothered Nancy, who nervously watched the speedometer, waiting for Ken to slow down. Not Ken. She looked up at him sweetly as a first-day bride should and said, "Honey, you are going too fast."

AN 80-MILE-AN-HOUR HUSBAND AND A 60-MILE-AN-HOUR WIFE

"Don't worry your pretty little self. You will get used to it." Just like easygoing Ken. He never slowed down. Imagine 60-mile-an-hour Nancy and 80-mile-an-hour Ken spending the rest of the day in that car. And there was another thing. Ken changed lanes often, darted between cars, and swooped around trucks. He was having a great time. But Nancy was having fits.

"Come to think of it, I have always given in to Ken," Nancy thought. She gave orders all day long at work. Ken's decisiveness had been a relief. She had enjoyed someone else making up her mind for her. But now . . . "Maybe he is just an inconsiderate person," she mused. "Will it always be like this?" As the car thundered on, she recalled many times when Ken had brushed aside her comments in his jolly way. Nancy spent the rest of the day protesting in her mind, mentally objecting to every rapid mile.

They stopped for lunch, and Nancy noticed something else about Ken. He was in a hurry to get back on the road, so he loaded his fork with food and gulped it down. Occasionally, he would hit his tooth with the fork. She had never noticed this until now, but the more she watched, the more disgusted she became. She sipped her iced tea properly. Across the table came a ping! A few minutes later, while she was cutting her steak . . . ping! While she was working on her vegetables . . . ping! Watching him gulp his food was bad. Listening to him chomp made it worse. Add an occasional ping, and lunch became unbearable.

She was rattled. There was first the difference of opinion over speed—the style of driving—and now Ken was chomping and "pinging" his way through the meal. A confused Nancy marched to the car. Ken hopped in and away they flew down the highway.

THE FIRST NIGHT

They came squealing up to the hotel at the end of the day. Another new experience awaited Nancy—her first time in a hotel with a man. And after a nerve-wracking day in the big, white BMW.

Ken walked into the room, unbuttoned his jacket, and let it fly. Nancy was the kind of person who always had a place for everything.

"Are you not going to hang your jacket up?"

"What?" A look of disbelief. "Hang my jacket up?" All he had ever done was aim his jacket at the nearest chair.

They made it to Miami in two-and-a-half days. Ken was hyper as they walked into the hotel on the evening of their third day of marriage. He threw open the drapes and peered out at the ocean lapping at the beach in the twilight.

"Wow! What a sight! Let's get up early and watch the sun rise over the ocean."

Nancy was completely worn out from nearly three days of tension. She was also angry, critical, and unresponsive. The ocean did not do anything for her, nor did Ken's suggestion. And Ken? He took it in stride.

"A good night's sleep will fix you up," he said. "It has been a long trip."

At 6:00 A.M. Ken was up, kissing Nancy awake. It was the last straw for her. "Leave me alone, Ken. I want to sleep," she told him angrily. He obliged and headed for the beach alone.

"Nothing like a brisk walk along the beach, bright and early," he said over his shoulder as he went out the door.

Nancy could not get back to sleep. She was wide awake and furious over his lack of consideration for her, mixed with shame over the harsh, bitter feelings toward him and her lack of responsiveness when he touched her.

In a tearful, emotional reunion, they promised each other that would never happen again. But as they discussed their differences, they found themselves in angry shouting matches or long silences. Ken was startled and surprised. After all, he was just being himself. It was a long drive back to Detroit.

So they ended up in my consulting room. Nancy was frightened at her hostility. Yet she became angry every time she retold the story. Embattled Ken could not believe his preoccupation but still excused his actions.

WHAT WAS THE PROBLEM?

Were they mismatched? Had they deceived each other from the beginning? Was there any hope? These were their anxious questions. I tried to lessen the tension.

"This is no serious problem," I assured them.

After all, Nancy was an executive who made decisions on her own all day long. She had her own apartment and for eight years had done whatever she pleased. The same was true with Ken. He, too, called the shots for his employees. After work he had gone his own way for years.

Two intelligent, free-thinking people—each accustomed to having other people carry out their wishes—had been thrown together. Two fine people discovered that working out a relationship involved making discoveries about each other and accommodating one another.

Ken had not known how upset Nancy had been. He was thoroughly enjoying himself. Nancy had no idea how firm Ken could be when he made up his mind.

Are Nancy and Ken an extreme case? Maybe. But there are many insensitive, highly motivated Kens around married to reluctant ladies, who have minds of their own.

Ken and Nancy sincerely wanted a loving, agreeable, and unselfish relationship. Yet, they missed it. Why?

The Bible offers a reason:

We have turned, every one, to his own way.
ISAIAH 53:6A

There it is. A simple housekeeping detail (hang up your coat) or a behavioral detail (punctuality) can turn a man and a woman into two angry, contentious opponents in a flash. Marriage can magnify rather then eliminate self-seeking.

I came across a few lines that say it well:

Oh, to dwell there above
With the saints that we love.
That will be glory!
But to dwell here below
With the saints that we know,
That is another story!

To be sure, heaven is a long-range goal. In the meantime, you work at living together here below. Ken and Nancy needed to live out esteeming others better than self.

I WILL SPEND MY LIFE PLEASING YOU

Before I married, I intended to be the most congenial, friendly, easygoing husband ever. I thought Eva would be the most congenial, friendly, easygoing wife. One night, during our courting days, she looked up into my eyes and said, "Henry, I will spend the rest of my life making you happy."

That rang the bell. Imagine, someone wanting to do that! For me? I bought that. I went even further.

"Eva, I will do the same for you." And I meant it. You can imagine what a tender night that was. We did not know we could not live up to those vows.

We went skiing on our honeymoon and got along fine. But we hit a snag the first night home. I went to visit the boys, as always. Nothing unusual or unpredictable. These men were my lifelong friends. For years we had gone skiing together, so that night we planned a weekend skiing trip. I went home and casually informed my wife, "I am going skiing over the weekend with the boys."

Remember her promise? This was her first chance to make me happy. She said, "No, you are not! You are married now!"

I was astonished, bewildered. I felt betrayed. Our first big conflict. It was quite a deal. We debated for several days before I finally got my way. No woman was going to tell me I could not go skiing!

What an attitude! It had not taken us long to discover that our commitment to make one another happy was a flimsy one. Our first few years together were stormy years, for we were using our respective creativity and intelligence to outmaneuver each other. Our intentions had been good, but not our ability to carry them out.

Many people need help these days. Every year the divorce statistics climb. In 1975, there were more than a million divorces for the first time in American history. Surely these million couples who divorced did not get married with the idea of fighting and hating the sight of each other.

On July 3, 1975, the headline on Ann Landers' column read, "Ann Has No Answer." In the column, she wrote:

> The sad incredible fact is that after thirty-six years of marriage, Jules and I are being divorced. As I write these words, it is as if I am referring to a letter from a reader. It seems unreal that I am writing about my own marriage . . .

That we are going our separate ways is one of life's ironies. How did it happen that something so good for so long did not last forever? The lady with all the answers does not know the answer to this one.

Perhaps there is a lesson there for all of us. At least there is for me. Never say, "It could not happen to us."

What sobering, chilling news. The divorce rate continues to climb.

THERE IS HOPE

Yes, it could happen to anyone.

Is there an answer? I think there is. It involves understanding how walls that lead to divorce are built—and understanding how to dismantle them and restore the pleasant, happy days of comfortable fellowship. It involves an examination of character.

RECOGNIZING REALITY

All married couples must face the same basic task. Two well-meaning people, accustomed to doing things a certain way, must develop a mutually agreeable and new way of life. The adjustments necessary during the honeymoon will be replaced by others again and again as life moves on.

WHAT WE DIDN'T KNOW

Nancy and Ken believed marriage would eliminate misunderstandings, loneliness, and emptiness. They received a rude awakening on their honeymoon.

My wife and I were jolted the day we came home from our honeymoon. We figured marriage would banish conflicts. No more problems with parents or brothers or sisters. We would do as we pleased and express ourselves freely. To our dismay, we clashed over a simple decision.

I have talked with thousands of couples, young and old alike, whose hopes for a happy marriage have been dashed. We discuss the same questions:

How is it possible—to feel so harshly toward someone you once felt such tenderness for? How is it possible—to be repulsed at the idea of being touched by a person who you once so desired that restraint was the constant problem? How is it possible—to have such sharp, unsolved conflicts when you once got along so well?

A MATTER OF WALLS

How? Why? It's a matter of walls. Invisible walls loom up and cut off affection, tenderness, and the will to work at your relationship as you did during dating days.

It even happens in those "perfect" marriages. Consider Susan and Greg. They had everything—housing, financial security, education, and a good background. Well, in just a few months, they were in my consulting room puzzling over the coldness that had wedged them apart.

She could not respond to his caresses, which was no problem the first few months of their marriage. So, why now? A wall had gone up—and a marriage was slowly coming down. Watch as Susan and Greg build this wall one incident at a time, just as a brick wall is built one brick at a time.

THEY DID THINGS RIGHT

It all started before marriage.

You could not find two more efficient people than Susan and Greg. He was a college graduate—handsome, talented, and neat. She had her bachelor's degree and was an excellent executive secretary. In addition, she was pleasant and beautiful.

Between them, they had saved enough money to build a house. So they spent their engagement looking for a building site, working on plans with an architect, and then actually building the house. This marriage was for keeps. When the house was built and furnished, the lawn in, and the driveway down, they were ready to get married. And they did.

Oh, there had been some debates over the building site and house plans—even over the furniture. But it was so much fun to make up after a quarrel. Flashes of anger were soothed with a gentle hug; a verbal tirade calmed with a tender kiss. Differences of opinion were carefully aired and settled. So it seemed.

Vaguely, Susan sensed the settlements usually ended up Greg's way. But then, he had such a logical mind. And her reasoning, well, sometimes it was not so good. Still, she liked some of those ideas even if she could not defend them. But she went along with Greg's reasoning and filed her ideas away.

To Greg, Susan seemed a bit illogical at times, but she caught on quickly. So he brushed aside his hardly noticeable irritability over her resistance to his ideas.

THE WALLS START BUILDING

Along here the wall begins. Only some of the issues were settled; only some of the anger appeared on the surface.

Susan opposed three changes in the house plans, but in the interest of peace (so she said), she let them pass. Consider her reluctant concessions as three invisible bricks. A number of Susan's ideas irritated Greg. They were so silly. But, in order to build a solid relationship, he suppressed his reactions and smiled—four invisible bricks.

That is how they started their marriage. It was the same old thing—hidden irritability . . . stubbornness . . . selfishness . . . that sequence that dooms so many marriages.

They did not realize that a thought tucked away and unspoken, an irritable spirit suppressed, and a critical attitude ignored build an invisible wall that slowly divides a couple. Each unresolved incident is another invisible brick. It cuts off the affection between them and cements in place tensions and thoughts unknown to each other.

Up to now, Greg and Susan had kept their true feelings and thoughts to themselves. Maybe it would not matter. Their situation was a dream come true. Even with these initial problems, it still had to be a super marriage.

THE GREAT INCIDENT

But it all came apart. All because of a little cobweb. Or so it seemed. The drama began one evening a few months after their beautiful wedding ceremony. Greg came home and he could not believe it! Of all things! There in the corner of the living room ceiling of his nice home was—a cobweb.

"Hmmm. She has not noticed it yet. I'll not say anything to her. She'll probably get it tomorrow." Another invisible brick. He did the standard things a young man should do when he comes home from work. He took Susan in his arms, kissed her, and told her how much he loved her.

The next evening, the cobweb was still there. Again, Greg took Susan in his arms, kissed her, and said, "I love you very much!"

And also the third evening. By the fourth evening—even though he was still hugging, kissing, and whispering sweet words—Greg was mad.

"There's that cobweb, doggone it. Doesn't she see it?" By the fifth evening, he was kissing her with his eye on the cobweb. And by the seventh, he was so disgusted he could hardly contain himself.

AND ON THE SEVENTH DAY, HE . . .

For six days Greg had added to the invisible wall that was made from the following:

1. Keeping his thoughts and feelings to himself
2. Deceiving his wife, pretending all was well

For six evenings he had kissed her, hugged her, and said the same words. Now it was the seventh evening, and the words were spilling out once again. "Susan, you're wonderful. I really love you. I'm glad we are married . . ." This time he broke off in mid-sentence. He couldn't go on with the act anymore. He'd finally gotten enough nerve.

"Susan," he said sweetly, though tentatively. "Do you see that cobweb? Do you know how long it's been up there? This is the seventh day."

Susan stepped back from the embrace, looked up, and discovered the cobweb. Now what do you think she said? What would you have said? Well, beautiful little Susan put her arms around Greg and answered, "Greg, I am glad I am married to you. You help me be a better woman." Then she kissed him and went to the kitchen to get a broom.

Greg felt like a heel. Look how mad he was and how nicely she took it. He ought to be ashamed of himself.

But he did not know Susan was not taking it well. All the way to the kitchen she was thinking, *Good grief, if it bothered him that much, why didn't he clean it up himself?* Maybe that thought occurred to you, too.

But when she came back to the scene of the cobweb with the broom, her manner was pleasant and she sweetly whisked the cobweb away.

Greg felt guilty. *What a sweet kid she is. I shouldn't have made such a fuss. But maybe I did help her. We don't want any cobwebs in the living room.*

THE EFFICIENCY EXPERT GOES TO WORK!

There were several weeks of peace around the house. *Silence* would be a better word because Susan was doing a slow burn over the "Great Cobweb Incident." But she did not act like it. Her manner toward Greg was beautiful. She had inadvertently spent two weeks adding to the wall between them. Her contribution?

1. Deception by pretending appreciation
2. Resentment

Then, one day, another incident. This time, it was about the way Susan was doing the dishes.

She was putting the dishes on a dish rack to dry (they had decided against getting a dishwasher). Greg, a professional efficiency expert, noticed something wrong. She was washing dishes cross-handed! In other words, she washed dishes with her right hand, then deposited them in the dish rack to her left.

"Honey," he said, "do you realize you are washing dishes cross-handed?" Then to lessen the sting, "Just a little tip to help you," followed by a nervous laugh. However, his uncertainty became scorn when Susan answered quizzically, "Cross-handed? What's that?"

He couldn't believe it! His wife didn't know what cross-handed was. So he showed her the "most efficient way to do dishes," explaining impatiently how it would be easier to put the dish rack to her right.

Do you know what Susan said? What would you have said? She wiped her hands on her apron, put her arms around her husband, and kissed him. "Greg, I appreciate that. I'd never have thought of it myself." Then she turned back to her dishes, doing them Greg's way.

Again, Greg felt terrible. He had been so disgusted, and she had been so nice. But he thought, *I think I did right. I really helped her.*

But that's not what Susan was thinking as she turned back to the dishes. "Oh brother!" she griped to the dishwater. "Is he going to tell me how to run my kitchen too?"

She stifled her protests and kept smiling, hugging, and kissing. Greg was encouraged and increased his "suggestions." After all, shouldn't you believe your wife's (or husband's) words? Over some weeks he had rearranged the cupboard, pantry, and other parts of the kitchen "more efficiently." Each time, Susan responded, as on cue, "Oh, thank you, Greg."

But her resentment grew with every comment.

WORKING TOGETHER . . . AT WHAT?

This contest went on for several months, with both Susan and Greg hard at work building their wall.

His contributions:

1. Deception . . . not sharing his thoughts
2. Impatience . . . toward her work habits
3. Disgust . . . with her "stupidity"

Her contributions:

1. Deception . . . pretending appreciation
2. Resentment . . . of his interference
3. Rebellion . . . making changes reluctantly

GREG MEETS A SUDDEN WATERLOO

Then came the crisis, the big battle. You guessed it . . . another cobweb. In the same living room, same corner. And he waited the same seven days, then repeated the earlier scene.

"Susan, do you know how long that cobweb has been there?" he asked, expecting a loving kiss, hug, and a thank you.

Fire replaced love in Susan's eyes. Her body bristled, and she stormed in all her fury, "I'm getting sick and tired of your suggestions! Why don't you mind your own business?"

Was he surprised!

We aren't, are we? We could see it coming all along. But not Greg. He had taken her at her word. He was not a mind reader. No one is. Greg recoiled—at his defensive best.

"OK, OK," he said. "I shouldn't have bothered you about it anyway. You've got every right to be mad."

It was a lie. This time He was pretending. *If she acts that way, I am certainly not going to help her anymore.* Now, both Susan and Greg were keeping their thoughts to themselves. And it got worse—so bad that I heard the story in my consulting room.

"We don't fight," she told me. "But there is tension. When his car pulls into the driveway, I find myself freezing up. I want to give him a warm welcome, but when he walks into the house, and I see his eyeballs sweep the ceiling, it turns me cold."

Their hugs were just so much bodily movement now. Their kisses were nothing more than a damp experience. Like the old song:

> There's a wall between us.
> It's not made of stone.
> The more we are together . . .
> The more we are alone.

THE CAUSE OF MOST SEX PROBLEMS

Like countless other couples, Susan and Greg were puzzled over their "sex problem." And they definitely had one. Susan froze up at the sight of Greg. Was he less manly now? Had she lost her normal desires? Not at all. They were both very much alive. She was as pretty, witty, and sensuous as ever. He was as handsome, stable, and virile as ever. They were divided by an invisible wall as real as if it were made of bricks. It was made out of familiar materials:

deception   rebellion
hatred   self-centeredness
resentment   impatience

WHAT HAPPENED?

Did the marriage create these reactions in Susan and Greg? No. Marriage *revealed* them. Jesus said,

> **"There is nothing that enters a man from outside
> which can defile him; but the things which come
> out of him, those are the things that defile a man."**
> MARK 7:15

But these people were educated, responsible, well-housed, well-clothed, and well-fed.

Yes. These benefits are highly desirable. However, they do not provide what you need to handle deception, hatred, resentment, rebellion, self-centeredness, or impatience.

THE EVERY-FEW-MONTHS BLOW-UP

Steve and Julie were five years into their marriage when I met them. Their relationship seemed good, at least compared to other marriages they knew about. They had much in common and had similar personalities. They were proud of their two small children. Their work with newlyweds at church was a source of great joy. Yet there was a problem that kept coming up. A wall had been constructed between them by their own hands. They were unable to see it until it was too late and they crashed into it, resulting in the "every-few-months blow-up."

It could start in a number of ways, usually something small, like plans for the weekend. Steve arrived home from work ready to relax and recover from a hard day. "Hi, Honey. I'm home," was his greeting. Julie, glad to see him, asked him about his workday and listened with interest as he related the events since he had left that morning. Sounds pretty good so far, doesn't it? The fireworks are just about to get underway. Notice that

> . . . with their mouth they show much love, *but* their hearts pursue their *own* gain.
> Ezekiel 33:31b

Julie was anxious to get the weekend planned since she likes to know what they will be doing to avoid wasting this precious family time. "Isn't it a beautiful day? I hear it's going to be this way all weekend. Let's go to the nursery Saturday morning and get some flowers to plant the front garden area. How about if we go out to that restaurant by the lake with some friends tomorrow night? I need to line up a babysitter now if we are going. What do you think?"

What man would not be thrilled to come home to a wife who is so excited about the weekend? After all, she went to all of the trouble to plan their activities; surely Steve would be thrilled. However, Steve is the kind of a guy who likes to have some unplanned time. His preference is to get up Saturday morning after sleeping late and do whatever comes to mind.

"Whoa. I'm tired, Julie. I just got back in town. Why do we always have to have something planned? I just want to relax. We'll see." Fuming,

Julie withdrew into the kitchen, slamming pots and pans as she prepared dinner. We see that someone

who isolates himself seeks his own desire;
He rages against all wise judgment.
PROVERBS 18:1

Now this issue of weekend plans in and of itself doesn't seem to be a big enough deal to precipitate a major problem between two people who love each other and truly enjoy each other's company. Yet it is surprising how such a small bump can liberate all of the grievances we hold in our cup. Steve followed her and asked what was wrong. "Oh, nothing," she said sweetly. We've all heard that before! *Well,* she thought, *if he doesn't care enough to know how I feel, I'm sure not going to spell it out!* Certainly,

The heart *is* deceitful above all *things,*
And desperately wicked;
Who can know it?
JEREMIAH 17:9

Then when Steve pressed her a few more times, Julie began to reel off all of the things she had been holding against him since the last big fuss. "You know I love being home with the kids, but just once in a while I wish we could go out. It's been over a month. And I walk by that pathetic garden every day. The weeds have taken over, and the spring rains have washed most of the good dirt away. The neighbors are starting to think that we just don't care how our property looks."

Steve met each charge as his own attorney for the defense, arguing passionately for his position with logic and skill, deflecting her accusations back at her in an effort to confuse and defeat her. "Don't you think I want to go out? We agreed that we were going to try and cut back on our spending this month. And besides, since when do we let our neighbors dictate to us how we spend our time and money? I agree these things need to be done, but we can't do everything in the same day."

Julie was ready with "I'm not expecting everything to be done on the same day. I've been talking about this for weeks and nothing is happening. You also agreed that we need to paint the house and update our budget. Yet somehow you found time to go on that rafting trip last weekend."

Now she had gone too far. Steve felt she was being ridiculous. "That's not fair. You're out of control. You encouraged me to go on that trip! Where is all of this coming from?" The answer becomes obvious in another question:

> **Where do wars and fights *come* from among you?**
> **Do *they* not *come* from your *desires for* pleasure**
> **that war in your members?**
> JAMES 4:1

At this point in the argument, the conversation wound up the "same old, same old" claims about one another. "I just want to make a plan. Is that so terrible? Why can't you ever take the initiative on something? Aren't you supposed to be the leader in our home?" Julie asks.

"Look, I work hard to make a good living for us. Don't I get any credit for that? You are way out of line here!" Steve would retort.

"I can never say anything when you're in a bad mood like this. You need to get right with God," would be Julie's response.

Now comes the ultimate in Steve's repertoire of exasperated comebacks. "I guess I should just realize from the beginning that everything is always my fault, Miss Perfect. How can you be so judgmental? You're unbelievable!" They illustrated that

> **A fool has no delight in understanding,**
> **But in expressing his own heart.**
> PROVERBS 18:2

When Julie's irritations met Steve's anger, the bricks they hurled at each other built a wall neither of them could see across. Soon anger was obviously a much bigger problem than the original difference of opinion, and the focus changed.

Finally, tired of fighting and satisfied that they had each made their points, they would make up. One would call a truce, and they would make some decision about the original disagreement. "I'm going for a drive. Why do you have to get so mad? Your ranting and raving is scaring me," Julie would say.

Steve would soften. "No, I'll not let you walk out of this house."

Then Julie in tears would say, "Okay, just don't get so defensive. I'm not making some big statement that you are a bad husband."

He knew she really loved him. "Okay, but it seems that way. I am sorry I got mad."

Julie implored, "Can we stop this now? We'll just stay home Saturday."

Pulling her into his arms, Steve offered, "I'll get my paperwork done early and we'll work on the budget while the kids watch cartoons. Then we'll know how much we can spend at the nursery on that front garden."

She kissed him. "Thanks."

Steve and Julie realized with shame that it did not merit the time and bother they had invested. They had removed some of the bricks, but the real problem of the wall of their self-centeredness remained. And they kept running into it every few months.

BIG WALLS COME FROM LITTLE BRICKS

Incredible, isn't it, that people get so distressed over driving, neatness, eating habits, time, and housekeeping? But we do. One incident does not mean that much, but the daily grind takes its toll. Picking up a towel that we threw carelessly at the tub is not so bad once. Even four times a day, twenty-eight times a week can be tolerated. But four times a day for six months? After a while, you start resenting it.

LITTLE ISSUES?

Think of the little issues that can pile up around the house. Start with the living room.

- What do you do with the newspaper? Fold it neatly on the coffee table? Or leave it strewn around the room, a section here, a section there?
- When you come home from work, do you change clothes before you sit down in the living room? Or lounge around with your grubby clothes on?

Let's move into the bedroom.

- How cool do you set the air conditioner? How high do you open the windows?
- How many blankets do you sleep under?
- Do you undress with the blinds down and the lights on? Or leave the blinds up and undress in the dark?

Take the bathroom.

- What do you do with wet towels? Drape them over the shower curtain? Over the bathtub? Put them in the clothes hamper? Or hang them neatly on the rack?
- Do you install the toilet paper with the paper coming down from the top or up from the bottom of the roll?
- Where do you put the toothbrushes?
- Do you start on a new tube of toothpaste before you've squeezed the old tube flat? How do you squeeze the tube?

Move into the dining room.

- Do you keep the different foods separated on your plate or mix them together?
- How do you serve the mustard and catsup? In bottles or in pretty little dishes?
- How do you cut the meat? Slice off a bite, eat it, then slice off another bite? Or cut the entire piece into many small bites first and then eat it?
- What about breakfast cereal? Pour the milk on first or sprinkle the sugar first?
- How do you appear for breakfast? All dressed? Or in your bathrobe?

One disagreement does not amount to much. Enough of them over a period of months build an invisible, divisive wall. We can compare it to constructing a building. One brick is hardly noticeable. Enough bricks make an enclosure that keeps you out.

In the consulting room, I hear many a puzzled partner say, "We are just not close anymore." "I can't stand him even touching me. There's nothing of value between us."

These are statements made by people who once thought marriage to that same person was a great idea.

BIGGER ISSUES

Perhaps you married with one or more widely varied views on life:
- Family of origin—hers is close and open, his is cool and distant
- Temperament—she is a risk-taker, he is very careful
- Political—she is liberal, he is conservative
- Cultural—she is Hispanic, he is Oriental
- Religious—she is Catholic, he is Protestant

In the thrill of romance during dating, the differences may have been ignored. After marriage you are apt to declare that you do not want to give up who you are. The bricks are laid in place between you.

REACTIONS TO OPINIONS ARE THE KEY

The clashes discussed so far involved differences of opinions between marriage partners. Their reactions to these clashes erected invisible walls that short-circuited the tenderness, fellowship, and will to make the partnership grow. It happens to newlyweds, old-timers, the educated, the wealthy, the healthy, the uneducated, the sick, and the poor.

No one gets married planning madness. All of the dreaming and planning is about growing closer and more intimate, not about building walls of isolation between each other. We anticipate warm glances and friendly greetings, not cold stares and sarcastic remarks. We dream of fun family vacations, not dealing with disobedient children. We claim to have found a soulmate, not an opponent. Where does this ship sailing toward marital bliss run onto the shoals of anger, bitterness, and estrangement?

To the single person, marriage is often viewed as a destination. Just getting there will be the key to living happily ever after. Soon after arrival, however, the destination turns into a journey, one filled with the possibilities of great happiness as well as the potential for great pain.

The journey at first seems mysterious, with many unexplained twists and turns that make you ill at ease. Soon, seeking to put some order into the situation, you construct a set of rules to live by. This is designed to prevent surprises so that you will always know what to expect from one another. But when the rules fail in their guarantee of happiness and the avoidance of pain, it becomes obvious that marriage must be about something more than rules.

From where I sit after eighty years of living, counseling, and being married most of those years, it is clear that though there is mystery, it is merely the mystery of the human heart. The heart is forever turning to its own way. The journey is itself a series of destinations: to remain Christlike, to communicate, to be like-minded, and to live out the proper roles, depending on God to lead and empower every step of your way.

There is a common thread running through the illustrations we have given you.

We have turned, every one, to his own way.
Isaiah 53:6a

Ken and Nancy valued their independence. It was more desirable than making the changes necessary to live together. They tried counseling, talking with clergy, and making many decisions among themselves. They decided to go their separate ways.

My wife and I, Greg and Susan, and Steve and Julie all recognized the sin of selfishness. We turned God-ward with repentant hearts and let the Lord cleanse our hearts and fill them with His Spirit. The invisible walls that divided us were quickly dismantled. Then followed a lifetime of practicing the principles in this book, one day at a time.

CHAPTER 2

Building Blocks for Marriage

In order to contribute your share to a mutually satisfactory marriage, you must be at peace with yourself. The pathway to personal peace is clearly marked for you in the Bible.

A lawyer once asked the Lord Jesus a question:

> **"Teacher, which is the great commandment
> in the law?"**
> MATTHEW 22:36

If you were to answer that question, which commandment would you select?

Contained in His answer are the building blocks that will provide a foundation that will sustain a wholesome marriage.

FIRST BUILDING BLOCK

The Lord's answer:

> Jesus said to him, " 'You shall love the LORD your
> God with all your heart, with all your soul, and
> with all your mind.' This is *the* first and great
> commandment."
> MATTHEW 22:37–38

The Lord Himself said that the single most important choice you will make in your lifetime is to live by the first great commandment. The first step in finding peace within yourself is to declare and demonstrate your love for God.

Jesus told His disciples how to demonstrate their love for Him:

> "If you love Me, keep My commandments."
> JOHN 14:15

> "He who has My commandments and keeps them,
> it is he who loves Me. And he who loves Me will
> be loved by My Father, and I will love him and
> manifest Myself to him."
> JOHN 14:21

Your love for God will be demonstrated by the place that His commandments occupy in your life. You must study His Word to learn what His commandments are.

To follow God's Word as life's guidebook requires a familiarity with the commandments and a keen sense of the place that they have in God's order. As an example, let us review what Jesus said about foundations:

> "Therefore whoever hears these sayings of Mine, and
> does them, I will liken him to a wise man who built his

house on the rock: and the rain descended, the floods came, and the winds blew and beat on that house; and it did not fall, for it was founded on the rock.

"Now everyone who hears these sayings of Mine, and does not do them, will be like a foolish man who built his house on the sand: and the rain descended, the floods came, and the winds blew and beat on that house; and it fell. And great was its fall."

MATTHEW 7:24–27

A serious study of the Bible will give you an understanding of what God requires of you and what you can expect from God. Jesus said that one house stood because it was founded on a rock—not only hearing His sayings, but doing them. The other house fell because it was built on sand—hearing His words, but not doing them.

- The Bible is the guide to righteousness.
- The Bible is the guide to peace.
- The Bible is the guide to stability.

You make daily use of a mirror because you want your personal appearance to be acceptable. A daily look into the Bible to see the reflection of your life is equally beneficial. The contented person is one whose outward appearance and inner life are acceptable to God.

In his epistle, James reassures us:

> But he who looks into the perfect law of liberty
> and continues *in it,* and is not a forgetful hearer
> but a doer of the work, this one will be blessed in
> what he does.

JAMES 1:25

A natural tendency is to skip the mirror of God's Word. It is easier to go your own way, following any line of logic that justifies a burning passion.

The writer to the Hebrews describes the Bible as

> **a discerner of the thoughts and intents of the heart.**
> HEBREWS 4:12B

Approaching it with this attitude, you will be guided into finding and maintaining a realistic understanding of yourself, your attitudes, thoughts, feelings, and desires. The psalmist expresses the attitude that leads to understanding of self:

> **Search me, O God, and know my heart;**
> **Try me, and know my anxieties;**
> **And see if *there is any* wicked way in me,**
> **And lead me in the way everlasting.**
> PSALM 139:23–24

GUIDE TO RIGHTEOUSNESS

A well-trained driver will almost automatically do the right thing at the right time in a car when under pressure. His "instinct" is a compound of knowledge and practice. In the Christian life, a knowledge of righteousness is basic to living righteously. Our sourcebook is the Bible. As Paul puts it:

> **All Scripture *is* given by inspiration of God, and *is***
> **profitable for doctrine, for reproof, for correction,**
> **for instruction in righteousness.**
> 2 TIMOTHY 3:16

David said in the Psalms:

> **Through Your precepts I get understanding;**
> **Therefore I hate every false way.**

> **Your word *is* a lamp to my feet**
> **And a light to my path**
> PSALM 119:104–105

If you are vague about the requirements for personal Christian living as stated in the Bible, you will do well to examine your goals. Do you want to live righteously? Do you want someday to feel at ease in God's presence? If you do, the Bible will tell you how.

A GUIDE TO PEACE

A peaceful life is the evidence of a righteous life. A promise beautifully stated by the prophet Isaiah is,

> **The work of righteousness will be peace,**
> **And the effect of righteousness, quietness and**
> **assurance forever.**
> ISAIAH 32:17

The psalmist said,

> **Great peace have those who love Your law,**
> **And nothing causes them to stumble.**
> PSALM 119:165

A peaceful walk is one that can be made by faith in God's ability to provide for man's inability. When we walk by faith, Paul's testimony in his letter to the Philippians becomes our secret of stability:

> **Not that I speak in regard to need, for I have**
> **learned in whatever state I am, to be content: I**
> **know how to be abased, and I know how to**
> **abound. Everywhere and in all things I have**

learned both to be full and to be hungry, both to
abound and to suffer need. I can do all things
through Christ who strengthens me.

PHILIPPIANS 4:11–13

GUIDE TO STABILITY

Life is made up of varied experiences. There are times of favorable circumstances and times of trouble, stable and unstable times, surprises, and varieties of decisions. The stable person meets life in a reasonably predictable, peaceful, and dependable way. In speaking of the righteous man, David describes him thus:

The law of his God *is* in his heart;
None of his steps shall slide.

PSALM 37:31

THE SECOND BUILDING BLOCK

"And *the* second *is* like it: 'You shall love your
neighbor as yourself.'"

MATTHEW 22:39

Jesus said that to love your neighbor is equal in importance to loving God with all your heart and soul and mind. He said that your love for your neighbor depends on your opinion of yourself.

What does it mean to love yourself? It means that in the quietness of your own soul there is a consciousness that your response to life is acceptable to God and, therefore, to yourself. You can think about your behavior and say to yourself, "I believe God was pleased with what I said today, the tone of voice I used, the way I acted, the desires of my heart, the feelings that I had towards others, and the thoughts that occupied my mind." This is neither pride, nor conceit, nor selfishness. *Such behavior is a miracle.* Sincere repentance for sin and a hunger for God's strength provide a healthy, wholesome regard for an inner life that is a key that will enable you to love your neighbor.

How Can We Have Peace with Self?

Proper Speech

We use speech to communicate with the people in our lives. This is one way whereby others can know what is in our hearts. Knowing this, David prayed,

> **Let the words of my mouth and the meditation of**
> **my heart**
> **Be acceptable in Your sight,**
> **O Lord, my strength and my redeemer.**
> Psalm 19:14

Here is some biblical advice:

> **Pleasant words *are like* a honeycomb,**
> **Sweetness to the soul and health to the bones.**
> Proverbs 16:24

> **. . . let every man be swift to hear, slow to speak,**
> **slow to wrath.**
> James 1:19

> **A wholesome tongue *is* a tree of life,**
> **But perverseness in it breaks the spirit.**
> Proverbs 15:4

A soft answer turns away wrath,
But a harsh word stirs up anger.
PROVERBS 15:1

Is it not obvious that such conversation is necessary if we are to have a good opinion of ourselves?

On the negative side, the Bible cautions us:

But shun profane *and* idle babblings, for they will
increase to more ungodliness.
2 TIMOTHY 2:16

Do all things without murmuring and disputing.
PHILIPPIANS 2:14

Lying lips *are* an abomination to the LORD,
But those who deal truthfully *are* His delight.
PROVERBS 12:22

A newspaper columnist reported a conversation with a taxi driver. He said he had just taken two women to a hotel. He had picked them up in the suburbs, and all the way to town they were talking about two other women who were to meet them in front of the hotel for a cup of tea. "If those two other women had been standing at the curb without a stitch on, I would not be surprised," he said. "The ladies in my cab had stripped them down to their very souls during that ride."

"Do not misunderstand me," one of them was saying, "I love Margaret, but . . ." After that, Margaret emerged as about the most despicable female since Lady Macbeth. The other fare said she knew all this and she, too, loved Margaret as well as Lynn, for whom she would do almost anything in the world. "But," she continued, "it stands to reason that Lynn cannot be any better than Margaret since the two are so thick, and everybody knows that birds of a feather flock together."

When the cab reached the hotel, the two fares got out, rushed up to the two women standing under the marquee, hugged them, and squealed, "Darlings, you look wonderful! Oh, what fun to see you again!" And there were more fond embraces.

How could the two women possibly benefit from their destructive criticism followed by pretending they think well of them and love them? The biblical standard:

> **Where *there is* no wood, the fire goes out;**
> **And where *there is* no talebearer, strife ceases.**
> PROVERBS 26:20

How different such a conversation is from the standard that is set by Paul!

> **Let no corrupt communication proceed out of your**
> **mouth, but what is good for necessary edification,**
> **that it may impart grace to the hearers.**
> EPHESIANS 4:29

Our goal, then, as Christians, is to avoid the kind of communication that does not edify. We are to speak words that are constructive. One step toward inner peace and a sense of personal wholesomeness has been taken if you are able to review the day, knowing that your speech was acceptable to God because you have used words that edify and satisfy.

Proper Actions

Your love for God will influence your behavior. Paul says,

> **And *whatever* you do in word or deed, *do* all in**
> **the name of the Lord Jesus, giving thanks to God**
> **the Father through Him.**
> COLOSSIANS 3:17

When we have guests in our home, we see to it that our house is as clean and orderly as possible. We are consciously as polite and attentive to each other as possible. We do this even if the guest is a stranger. We notice that when we are guests in homes, the hosts do the same toward one another. They go out of their way to treat us like special people. Imagine how we would behave toward one another if the Lord dropped in for a visit. What changes would we make if He announced that for one week He would be at your side all your waking hours?

In the words of A. W. Tozer:

> We must offer all of our acts to God and believe that He accepts them; then hold firmly to that position and keep insisting that every act of every hour of every day and night be included. . . . Let us practice the fine art of making every work a priestly ministration. Let us believe that God is in all of our simple deeds and learn to find Him there.

When you love someone, that person is in the background of your thinking, even when you are apart. I was traveling in Kenya, Africa. My wife did not accompany me on that trip. Wherever we went I kept imagining in my mind how she would respond if she were there.

The one who loves God will have the goal of pleasing God in all that is done. The Bible describes the attitude that a God-loving person has toward any task:

> **And whatever you do, do it heartily, as to the**
> **Lord and not to men, knowing that from the Lord**
> **you will receive the reward of the inheritance; for**
> **you serve the Lord Christ.**
> COLOSSIANS 3:23–24

Jesus elaborated on how the one who loves God responds to a need:

**"For even the Son of Man did not come to be
served, but to serve, and to give His life a ransom
for many."**
MARK 10:45

The apostle Paul describes God's love in action:

Let no one seek his own, but each one the other's
well-being.
1 CORINTHIANS 10:24

The owner of a building supply company shared a beautiful story with me.

Eight years ago a young man showed up looking for work. This was a time of severe recession in the area. Jobs were almost non-existent. The only job available was the lowliest, dirtiest cleanup job in the sawmill. It was so undesirable that the management could not keep anyone, even though jobs were scarce. The last man who was hired had just quit, so the job was open. The young man was hired on the spot.

He started out optimistically like all the rest. Unlike the rest he seemed to relish the job. After several months, the longest anyone stayed, he had found ways to do the job better and faster. Instead of needing eight hours a day, he only needed six hours. Instead of leaning on his broom and complaining, he was asking for more work instead of a raise. His explanation for such outstanding performance was that he was just doing the best he could to earn his money because he was a Christian. Other work was soon found for him to do.

To bring the story up to date, he now is responsible

for running the sawmill and material handling in our retail outlets. His explanation for his performance is that God delivered him from a mean disposition that threatened to destroy his marriage and hindered his progress socially and professionally. He says he wants to please God who loves his boss. Since the man also loves his boss, he puts his heart in his work as he serves the company.

I am writing this delightful story from Horn Creek Conference Center, located just outside Westcliff, Colorado. In 1950, Paul and Jean Zeller started out to develop a Christian camp for kids. They purchased 160 acres of land in a remote wilderness area for $10 an acre. They had $500 to put down and not a dime for development. They borrowed $1,100. Today it is a haven for those who want to spend some time in a Christian environment in an unspoiled corner of the Rocky Mountains. Their purpose is to serve people in the name of the Lord. Sure enough, when we arrived at the Center, Jean was there to greet us in her predictable, courteous manner. When we got to our room, there was Paul cleaning rooms for new arrivals. These are the founders and directors. They were filling in so that some staff could have a day off. They are walking examples of people who seek the good of others.

How wonderful to enjoy what you are doing and to do it heartily as an act of worship! This should be true whether your work is at the desk, at the beach, in the shop, behind the pulpit, or in the home. The poet has aptly put this thought into words:

> Let me but do my work from day to day,
> In field or forest, at the desk or loom,
> In roaring market place or tranquil room;
> Let me find it in my heart to say,
> When vagrant wishes beckon me astray,
> This is my work; my blessing, not my doom;
> Of all who live, I am the one by whom

This work can best be done in the right way.
Then shall I see it not too great, nor small,
To suit my spirit and to prove my powers;
Then shall I cheerful greet the laboring hours.
And cheerful turn, when the long shadows fall
At eventide, to play and love and rest,
Because I know for me my work is best.
—HENRY VAN DYKE

The Bible gives you a standard for measuring many of your actions:

**All things are lawful for me, but all things are not
helpful. All things are lawful for me, but I will not
be brought under the power of any.**
1 CORINTHIANS 6:12

**All things are lawful for me, but not all things are
helpful; all things are lawful for me, but not all
things edify. Let no one seek his own, but each one
the other's *well-being*.**
1 CORINTHIANS 10:23–24

Every act of every day, every simple deed, is or is not an act of obedience to God. As you retire at night and meditate upon the day, you will
realize that the quality of the multitude of deeds done that day will determine whether God could say to you,

"'Well *done*, good and faithful servant.'"
MATTHEW 25:21A

**And let us not grow weary while doing good, for
in due season we shall reap if we do not lose heart.**
GALATIANS 6:9

THE DESIRE OF THE HEART

God's promise to Israel long ago has a message for us today:

"If you are willing and obedient,
You shall eat the good of the land."
ISAIAH 1:19

A friend died recently of cancer. At one point, near the end of his life, he began to realize that he bitterly resented his lot in life. He reported that as he repented of his sin, he was cleansed. Then he requested that God fill him with peace and joy. He endured the rest of his illness in a quiet, peaceful, contented fashion. He said that enduring bitter resentment was worse than the pain caused by the cancer.

Daniel lived in an environment where all around him people were eating, drinking, and making merry. However, the record states,

But Daniel purposed in his heart that he would not defile
himself with the portion of the king's delicacies, nor with
the wine which he drank; therefore he requested of the
chief of the eunuchs that he might not defile himself.
DANIEL 1:8

If Daniel had secretly longed for the king's meat and wine, his abstinence would have been hypocrisy and deceit.

David asks the question and then answers it:

Who may ascend into the hill of the LORD?
Or who may stand in His holy place?
He who has clean hands and a pure heart,
Who has not lifted up his soul to an idol,
Nor sworn deceitfully.
He shall receive blessing from the LORD,
And righteousness from the God of his salvation.
PSALM 24:3–5

A young man was an outstanding leader in church activities during his high school days. To everyone's surprise, he quit following after spiritual things during his college days, even though he attended a Christian university. He began indulging in activities frowned upon by his church. He discontinued going to church, Bible study meetings, and youth rallies. The reason? He said his heart had never been in his church activities. Now he was doing what he had always longed to do. Your desires need to be in accord with your words and actions if you wish to find inner peace.

THE OUTER MAN MUST AGREE WITH THE INNER MAN

There is much social pressure that requires you to look happy, to act as if you were happy, to be polite, and to do the acceptable thing. The Christian is concerned not only with his tone of voice, but with what is in the heart as well; not only with how he acts, but with how he feels. The Bible says,

> But if you have bitter envy and self-seeking in
> your hearts, do not boast and lie against the truth.
> This wisdom does not descend from above, but *is*
> earthly, sensual, demonic.
> JAMES 3:14–15

To illustrate, a certain woman is friendly, easy to talk to, and likable. Consequently, she is often invited to neighbors' homes for coffee. Friends often ask her to drive them somewhere. The church is often asking her to do special tasks. Her husband frequently brings guests home.

But behind her friendly manner is her dislike of people and resentment because she feels that she is being imposed upon. The people who call upon her surely benefit from her services and her friendliness. She is the loser. The conflict between her acting and feeling brought on by the demands made on her time causes her endless misery.

A reporter tells of a reaction common to many. While covering a dog show, he approached an official for a press pass, explaining that he wanted to write an article about the show. The official delivered a brief, snarling lecture on the subject of people who expect to get into dog shows free, unless they are showing dogs. Then he asked, "Are you showing dogs?" "No, I am not!" replied the reporter. The official abruptly turned his back, leaving an astonished and overwhelmed reporter. Immediately the newsman began to think of things he should have said. Sharp-edged retorts leaped into his mind. He fancied a much more successful comeback that included side-stepping an irate, lunging official and flooring him with a neat right to the jaw. He had thought himself into a sweat before something else took his attention.

The Bible graphically describes the reporter's response:

> *The words* of his mouth were smoother than butter,
> But war *was* in his heart;
> His words were softer than oil,
> Yet they *were* drawn swords.
> PSALM 55:21

Physicians tell us that hostility, jealousy, anger, rage, resentment, and envy are some of the reactions that can cause such problems as disorders of the gastrointestinal tract, disorders of the heart, disorders of the skin, and headaches. The miraculous development of medicines has proven to be very effective in calming such reactions. The psychologist calls these reactions emotions.

According to psychiatrists and psychologists, these same reactions can also result when the patient has been mistreated by people or subjected to adverse circumstances. They declare these to be normal reactions that can be managed by human intelligence, education, and proper human interaction. Poorly managed reactions require the aid available through psychiatry and/or psychology. Skilled therapists can assist you. If necessary, a carefully administered drug program can help. It can take as much as two years or more for a therapist to help you understand how to manage your reactions caused by past and present experiences. It is comforting to know that the terrible discomfort can be relieved with medication and therapy. Again, such reactions are called emotions.

A DILEMMA

What is a Bible student to do with this information? The Bible declares the same emotions—hostility, jealousy, anger, rage, resentment, and envy—to be acts of the sinful nature. Only God can help if it is sin. Jesus said,

> "What comes out of a man, that defiles a man. For
> from within, out of the heart of men, proceed evil
> thoughts, adulteries, fornications, murders, thefts,
> covetousness, wickedness, deceit, licentiousness, an
> evil eye, blasphemy, pride, foolishness. All these evil
> things come from within and defile a man."
> MARK 7:20–23

The second example is the apostle Paul's writing. Notice these acts are evident, or obvious.

> Now the works of the flesh are evident, which are:
> adultery, fornication, uncleanness, licentiousness,
> idolatry, sorcery, hatred, contentions, jealousies,
> outbursts of wrath, selfish ambitions, dissensions,
> heresies, envy, murders, drunkenness, revelries, and
> the like; of which I tell you beforehand, just as I also
> told *you* in time past, that those who practice such
> things will not inherit the kingdom of God.
> GALATIANS 5:19–21

What is a Bible student to do with this verse?

> **If we say that we have no sin, we deceive our-
> selves, and the truth is not in us. If we confess our
> sins, He is faithful and just to forgive us *our* sins
> and to cleanse us from all unrighteousness.**
> 1 JOHN 1:8–9

The Bible declares that God will purify us of these so-called human emotions. They are sins. Only God can help us. God is the source of supernatural help in facing the dilemma. God says,

> **Walk in the Spirit, and you shall not fulfill the lust
> of the flesh.**
> GALATIANS 5:16

> **But the fruit of the Spirit is love, joy, peace, long-
> suffering, kindness, goodness, faithfulness, gentle-
> ness, self-control. Against such there is no law.**
> GALATIANS 5:22–23

The psychologist calls these emotions.

Jesus modeled a spiritual response to the problems that come our way. Peter said of the Lord Jesus,

> **who, when He was reviled, did not revile in return;
> when He suffered, He did not threaten, but com-
> mitted *Himself* to Him who judges righteously.**
> 1 PETER 2:23

He called upon God, saying,

> **"Father, forgive them, for they do not know what
> they do."**
> LUKE 23:34

YOUR GOAL—A WHOLESOME RESPONSE

The circumstances do not determine our response. What a relief. The choice is yours whether to yield your life to the Spirit or not.

Such talk is nonsense to the humanist, who by faith declares there is no God. To the humanist, the concept of sin is to pile a load of unnecessary guilt on top of an already troubled person.

This is a fork in the road. Which way will you turn for help? If it is sin you are dealing with, only God can cleanse you. If it is relief you seek, then you can turn to the world around you for help.

Words and deeds, without appropriate desires and feelings behind them, leave you cold and dissatisfied with yourself. You are kept from a proper love of your neighbor.

Each of us has his private world of thoughts. The questions are often asked: "What do you think of that person?" "What do you suppose he meant?" "What did you think of the sermon?" Such questions illustrate that you hold the key to the gate of your thoughts. No one can share your thoughts without your consent. In order for you to have a sense of wholesomeness, you must experience wholesome thinking.

Your goal ought to be that your response to the unexpected situation—the unfair, unreasonable situation—will be a wholesome, positive, and spiritual response:

> . . . casting down arguments and every high thing that
> exalts itself against the knowledge of God, bringing every
> thought into captivity to the obedience of Christ . . .
> 2 CORINTHIANS 10:5

When you achieve this goal, you will find that your thoughts will conform to the exhortation of Philippians 4:8:

> Finally, brethren, whatever things are true, what-
> ever things are noble, whatever things *are* just,
> whatever things *are* pure, whatever things *are*

lovely, whatever things *are* of good report, if *there
is* any virtue and if *there is* anything
praiseworthy—meditate on these things.

SUMMARY

Spiritually motivated words, actions, desires, feelings, and thoughts are the ingredients that give you a sense of personal wholesomeness. These qualities are necessary in order that you might love your neighbor as yourself.

No doubt, as you finish this chapter you may feel overwhelmed. Who can measure up to such a standard?

It would take a miracle to live like this.

Exactly. Read on.

CHAPTER 3

The Love of God Is the Pacesetter for Marriage

[Part of this chapter is written by Dr. Henry T. Blackaby.
We have left his words separate from our writing.]

Henry T. Blackaby

The love of God must be the pacesetter for your love for each other and your love for your children. Why? Because there will come moments when you differ with one another. It is absolutely crucial how you deal with those who differ with you. Remember a situation in your life where you felt that someone was mistreating you, or acted in a godless way toward you? If you did not stand guard over your heart, you probably considered them your enemy at that time. Jesus said nothing from the outside of you can affect your heart, because your heart is under your control.

> And He said, "What comes out of a man, that
> defiles a man. For from within, out of the heart of
> men, proceed evil thoughts, adulteries,
> fornications, murders . . ."
> MARK 7:20–21

What is on the outside cannot affect the inside because you are in control of that. So no one can make you bitter. They created the opportunity for you to be bitter, and you took it. The condition of your heart was revealed, not the condition of theirs. Five minutes with bitterness in your heart is too costly. Not only will it cost you, it will also cost your children.

If you consider someone as your enemy, how does Jesus tell you to treat them? Jesus said to love them.

> **"But I say to you, love your enemies, bless those**
> **who curse you, do good to those who hate you,**
> **and pray for those who spitefully use you and**
> **persecute you."**
> MATTHEW 5:44

This is God's plumb line—His standard. If you have anybody whom you are angry and bitter toward, it does not matter whether it comes from your childhood, from abuse or neglect, brokenness, or anything else. The question is not, "Where did it come from?" The question must be, "Are you doing what Jesus told you to do?" Loving your enemies is a command. Do you love your enemies? You say, "Well, I can't do it." God says, "That's right. Only I can do it." God wants you to stay close to Him because He will love people in your life and through your life. When God does this, the whole world will wonder where in the world that kind of love came from.

Jesus also said to pray for your enemies. Do you have a separate page in your prayer journal for your enemies? Surely you would not want to hear God tell you what to do with them without being very careful to obey Him.

Jesus also said to do good to your enemies. That means that you find opportunities without any initiative from others to do something very special toward them. Are you doing that? Jesus also said to bless them. You are to love them, you are to pray for them, you are to do good to them, and you are to bless them.

Does that sound terrible to you? It does not sound bad to God. How different are you from the world if you treat people the same way the world would? The world hates its enemies, so you are not being any different if you act like it. Do you only give to those who give back to you? Do you only bless those who bless you? Jesus desires that you go beyond what the world does, and do to others what God did for you.

> **But God demonstrates His own love toward us, in that while we were still sinners, Christ died for us.**
> ROMANS 5:8

When you were His enemy, what did He do? What effect did God's love have on you? It made His enemies His friends. You came to love Him because He first loved you. God takes the initiative to love. In the same way that God loves you, He wants you to love. You should take the initiative in loving people. Are you waiting for someone else to say, "Forgive me" or "I love you"? Do you take the initiative? Again, our problem is not that we do not know what to do; the problem is that we do know what to do, but we will not do it.

When one of our children went away from the Lord, flunked the tenth grade, and got in with the wrong crowd, I had some very sensitive people who gave me counsel. It is amazing how many people want to tell you what to do when you have a real problem. There was a fad going through the Christian community about that time called "Tough Love." "Tough Love" meant that you needed to be fair, honest, and open with your children. You must set some biblical guidelines for the home. Then you need to say to the child, "These are the guidelines that we must have in our home. If you're not willing to follow them, then you will have to leave." Well, it made sense until I went before God. When I went before God, He reminded me that He had rules in His house and I broke every one of them—yet He did not kick me out of His house. God forgave me and forgave me and forgave me. Now go and forgive your child also. Does that make sense?

Many say, "But, Lord, I forgave seven times!" But God said,

"I do not say to you, up to seven times, but up to
seven times seven."
MATTHEW 18:22

Human reasoning reminds you that you have been hurt and that you have no more mercy and forgiveness. It's their turn. You can do it that way if you want and lose your family, or you can do with your family what God did with you—keep forgiving.

Forgiveness will always cost the one who forgives far more than it costs the one being forgiven. Christ did not deserve the cost but He chose to pay the cost. When Christ created the opportunity for you to be forgiven, it cost Him far more than it did you. Many want to emulate Jesus when He was teaching the multitudes, preaching, and healing, yet not many want to be like the picture of Christ in Isaiah 53 that pictures a suffering servant. Jesus was despised, and rejected of men. He was a man of sorrows and thoroughly acquainted with grief. He was despised, and we did not esteem Him at all. Surely He has borne our grief and carried our sorrows. We thought He was stricken, smitten of God, and afflicted. But He was wounded for our transgressions. He was bruised for our iniquities. The chastisement that was required to bring us peace was upon Him, and with His stripes we are healed. Do you still want to be like Jesus?

Once I read that passage, God asked me to take all those verses and put a blank line by every phrase and every word. Then the Lord instructed me that if I had an honest heart before Him, I would put a date in that blank line when I was willing to be like that. As I began, it was one of the most difficult times in my life. My heart wanted to be like Jesus, but now I had the complete picture of what that meant. And the Lord kept reminding me, "Henry, that's what was taking place in your Savior because He loved you even though you never understood."

Christ's love is the pattern for love. I discovered that there was no possibility of being the kind of father or husband that I needed to be if I did not take His love as the pattern.

There is a verse that I still have to ask the Spirit of God to teach me.

> **Yet it pleased the LORD to bruise Him;**
> **He has put *Him* to grief.**
> **When You make His soul an offering for sin,**
> **He shall see *His* seed, He shall prolong *His* days,**
> **And the pleasure of the LORD shall prosper in His**
> **hand.**
> ISAIAH 53:10

It pleased the Lord to bruise Him. I did not understand how it could please God to bruise His Son. How could God say that and be perfect love? The last part of the verse says that He put Him to grief, and He made His soul an offering for sin. Have you ever known of a love like that? The world knows nothing of that kind of love. The world is selfish and self-centered. You may think, "If it causes pain in me, I'm going to strike back. I'm going to get out of it; I don't think I deserve this." The Lord did not deserve to die either, but He did.

Your marriage will only be as strong as you are willing to be like your loving Lord. Will there come difficult times? Will there be times of bewilderment? Will there be times of pain and misunderstanding? Will there be times of grief? Yes.

I was at a conference center one summer and a young lady who seemed to be in her 30s asked if she could speak with me. She was a beautiful young lady, radiant with joy. What she said next, I was totally unprepared for. She looked at me and smiled and said, "God gave me three beautiful children, and I've lost all three, and I can't have any more children." She began to describe how her children died at different times and different ages. She went through a gracious time with the Lord. She said, "I'm so profoundly grateful that God gave me those children. I would rather have loved them and lost them than to have never loved at all. God has left in my heart an incredible dimension of loving, and now He's said, 'There are a whole lot of folk out there who are hurting, and they don't have My love in their hearts like you do. And when they lose a child, it may shatter their marriage. And when they lose a child, it's going to be tough on them. I'll put you alongside of them.' I don't think I would ever have had the wonder of the ministry God's given me if He hadn't taken my three children."

I hung my head in shame. Nobody can ever love like that unless they understand how they have been loved. But when God loves us, it creates a capacity to love like Him. But the world does not know anything about that.

God's people, in the stress and strain of their marriages, must simply love one another the way God loved us. Have you ever been forgiven? Have you ever had to ask God to forgive you?

The Lord's Prayer gives a perfect example of forgiveness. Have you recently asked God to forgive you of anything—word or deed or thought, or what you did not do that you should have done? When you asked God to forgive you, did you pray something like this: "Oh Father, I've sinned against You. It's not what You've asked—I've left undone—Oh God, I want You to forgive me, but Lord, I want You to forgive me in exactly the same way I'm forgiving those who sin against me." That is exactly what Jesus said!

> **"For if you forgive men their trespasses, your
> heavenly Father will also forgive you. But if you
> do not forgive men their trespasses, neither will
> your Father forgive your trespasses."**
> MATTHEW 6:14–15

It is amazing that many do not pray the way Christ taught us in the most fundamental prayer of the entire Bible. You should pray, "Father, forgive me in the same way in which I forgive those who sin against me." Have you ever felt your spouse did not act properly? If you did not forgive immediately, you probably chose to remember that fault. God puts your sin away as far as the East is from the West and remembers it no more—never brings it up again. Do you have a memory that remembers every sin your spouse ever committed? If you forgave, you would choose never to bring it up again.

There's a Scripture that has disciplined me. Jesus said,

> **"For with what judgment you judge, you will be judged; and with the same measure you use, it will be measured back to you."**
> MATTHEW 7:2

This passage ends the discussion. If you have a really difficult time in your prayer life, there may be a root cause. The root cause may be an unforgiving relationship. As long as you stay in that unforgiving attitude, you will have sin in your heart and the Lord will not hear you.

HOW CRITICAL IS IT FOR THE LORD TO HEAR YOUR PRAYER?

One day I noticed that Marilynn was very ill. It was shortly after our last child was born, and I rushed her to the hospital. The doctor took me aside and told me my wife was very critically ill and that he did not know if he could spare her. He said they would do their best but could not hold out hope for me. When those doors closed and they took Marilynn into the surgery room, it was one of the loneliest times in my life. What is a Christian and a child of God to do in a moment of utter helplessness? You cry unto God. How important was it that I have a clean relationship with the Lord when I cried unto Him for my wife? God does not play favorites, and He does not make exceptions. If there is sin that I have not dealt with, He will not hear me.

Many think that God will hear you if there is an emergency, but He does not make exceptions. When I went alone to that waiting room, I found myself in an incredible time of helplessness. I found myself crying out to God—then suddenly, just like that, great peace came over me. It was God saying, "My child, it is done; she's okay."

I learned how critical it was to recognize when God is speaking to me. After a while the doctor came out, took off his mask, and said, "Mr. Blackaby, I've got good news—your wife is going to be all right."

I said, "Sir, I know."

He said, "How do you know?"

I said, "My heavenly Father told me."

He said, "Well, He's the only one who could have known."

I looked at him with all the emotion in my heart and said, "Sir, in my life He's the only one who really counts." When He speaks, it is so.

How important is it in your marriage that you keep your life right with God? Will there be moments when you want to cry unto God in your helplessness? Would it be important to know that you have a clean heart before God?

Paul made a statement that has encouraged me:

> **For the love of Christ constrains us, because we judge thus: that if One died for all, then all died.**
> 2 CORINTHIANS 5:14

What was it that caused Paul to do the will of God? The love of God. It never crosses my mind that when God tells me something I need to be or something I need to do that the instruction isn't absolutely an expression of the love of Christ. God can guide you around the land mines of life.

The Lord helped me understand how important His Word is. My dad was in the First World War and in one of the terrible battles. He was a machine gunner. My dad was told to go across a minefield carefully. They sent someone with him who was an expert in detecting mines. Whatever the mine detector told him to do, he did. It was his life that was at stake! Back then they did not have any Velcro, but they would have named him

Velcro Blackaby. You see, he did not know where the land mines were, but the man who was guiding him did. And when he said stop, dad stopped. When he said carefully move to the left, he carefully moved to the left. Everything the man said, Dad did, and he got all the way over the minefield safely. The heavenly Father says, "There's a way that looks right out there. You look at the field and it looks perfectly innocent—but Henry, it's full of mines." If you get partway out there, you will not know how to recognize it—but God does.

When God tells you to obey Him, do it immediately. When God speaks about what to do in your love toward your spouse, it is not a time for discussion—do it immediately because it is your life. Cling to God.

> "For this commandment which I command you today, it *is* not *too* mysterious for you, nor *is* it far off. It *is* not in heaven, that you should say, 'Who will ascend into heaven for us and bring it to us, that we may hear it and do it?' Nor *is* it beyond the sea, that you should say, 'Who will go over the sea for us and bring it to us, that we may hear it and do it?' But the word *is* very near you, in your mouth and in your heart, that you may do it.
>
> "See, I have set before you today life and good, death and evil, in that I command you today to love the LORD your God, to walk in His ways, and to keep His commandments, His statutes, and His judgments, that you may live and multiply; and the LORD your God will bless you in the land which you go to possess. But if your heart turns away so that you do not hear, and are drawn away, and worship other gods and serve them, I announce to you today that you shall surely perish; you shall not prolong *your* days in the land which you cross over the Jordan to go in and possess. I call heaven and earth as witnesses today against you, *that* I have set before you life and death, blessing and cursing;

therefore choose life, that both you and your descendants may live; that you may love the LORD your God,
that you may obey His voice, and that you may cling to
Him, for He *is* your life and the length of your days;
and that you may dwell in the land which the LORD
swore to your fathers, to Abraham, Isaac, and Jacob, to
give them."

DEUTERONOMY 30:11–20

The love of God is the pacesetter for the way we love one another,
but we are not ignorant of what that love is like—it is profound. You cannot love that way unless God helps you to love your spouse that way.

[Henry Brandt and Kerry Skinner finish the chapter from this point forward.]

LOVE IS MORE THAN A TINGLE

What is it that binds two people together in marriage? During
courtship, all couples reassure each other that love will carry them
through anything. When I press troubled couples to define love, the
answer is always the same: tender feelings and words, sincere promises, a
thrilling response to hugs and kisses, ecstatic response to sexual relations
shared exclusively by husband and wife and kept alive by each other.

They soon discover that disagreements lead to harsh words and ill
will. These disagreements cool the thrill and ecstasy of physical contact.
They often tell me they have lost their love.

Frequently, someone comes to see me greatly disturbed. This person
loves someone else, not the marriage partner. They have discovered that
"love" is not limited to an exclusive relationship with the marriage partner.

It is of critical importance to define what you mean by love. Jesus
Himself said,

> "'You shall love the LORD your God with all your
> heart, with all your soul, and with all your mind.'
> This is *the* first and great commandment."
> MATTHEW 22:37–38

Assuming you have declared your love for God, how do you demonstrate that love? Jesus told us how:

> "He who has My commandments and keeps them,
> it is he who loves Me. And he who loves Me will
> be loved by My Father, and I will love him and
> manifest Myself to him."
> JOHN 14:21

Some of the benefits of mastering the commandments are:

> Your word *is* a lamp to my feet
> And a light to my path.
> PSALM 119:105

> The law of his God *is* in his heart;
> None of his steps shall slide.
> PSALM 37:31

In the upper room, following the last supper that Jesus was to have with His disciples, He gave them final instructions. He said,

> "A new commandment I give to you, that you love
> one another; as I have loved you, that you also
> love one another. By this all will know that you
> are My disciples, if you have love for one
> another."
> JOHN 13:34–35

In writing to the Thessalonians, Paul makes a further demand on your love, and he leaves no doubt about the source of that love:

> **And may the Lord make you increase and abound in**
> **love to one another and to all, just as we *do* to you.**
> 1 Thessalonians 3:12

The apostle John adds,

> **Beloved, let us love one another, for love is of**
> **God; and everyone who loves is born of God and**
> **knows God.**
> 1 John 4:7

A New Resource

Here is the good news:

> **Now hope does not disappoint, because the love**
> **of God has been poured out in our hearts by the**
> **Holy Spirit who was given to us.**
> Romans 5:5

The love that produces harmonious living is not generated between people. It comes from outside yourself and starts with God's love. Whether you received Christ long ago or just today, you have access to His love. Ask Him to bathe your heart with it. You will be amazed at the change in your reactions to your partner. But you need to know what you are asking for.

The Oil That Eliminates Friction: God's Love

If you would take a sample of crude oil and break it down into its elements, you would get a variety of products including:

Kerosene	Ethane
Gasoline	Propane
Methane	Butane
Grease	Lubricating oils

Likewise, the love of God can be broken into its elements. The Bible does this in 1 Corinthians 13:4–7. In that Scripture passage (adapted from LB), God says:

- Love is patient and kind.
- Love is never jealous or envious.
- Love is never boastful or proud.
- Love is never haughty or selfish or rude.
- Love does not demand its own way.
- Love is not irritable or touchy.
- Love does not hold grudges.
- Love will hardly even notice when others do it wrong.
- Love is never glad about injustice.
- Love rejoices when truth wins out.
- Love is loyal no matter what the cost, always believes in others.
- Love expects the best of others.
- Love stands its ground in defending others.

It is a human impossibility to live up to this list. Notice also that sexual behavior or response is not on the list. Since drawing upon the love of God is so important, let's take a long look at it so you can know how He can help.

LOVE IS PATIENT (LONGSUFFERING)

It is the love of God in you that determines whether you will respond patiently or impatiently.

One couple was driven into my consulting room by their impatience.

"If we've told our son once, we've told him a hundred times to clean up his room. He's driving us up a wall. Patience doesn't work. When we run out of patience, we make him do it. Impatience is what works."

My answer?

Your son's choice reveals your impatience, not your patience. You impatiently allowed him to keep a messy room, and then you impatiently made him clean it up. *You think inaction is evidence of patience, and action is evidence of impatience.* Not so. You lack patience whether you make him do it or allow him not to do it. You are confusing patience with supervision. Any businessman knows that he must provide daily supervision to assure that his employees do what is required. The old rule of thumb is that the employee will do what the boss *inspects,* not what he expects.

If adults need daily supervision, how much more do children need it! All of us tend to go our own way, including children. The patience you need while you supervise your child is available to you from God.

How do you get it? You admit you need it, repent, and ask God to bathe your heart with patience as you work with your son to get his room cleaned up.

Some people cannot find anyone to marry and are miserable, yet in my consulting room I talk to people who suffer because they did find someone to marry.

"I've had enough. I can't stand it anymore!" my client says as though he is the only one who has trouble with a partner. Everybody does. Impatience is a common malady. Circumstances and the people in your life reveal it. What is the answer?

You can let God bathe your heart with love that exudes patience. Your problem does not go away, but you can think straight and quietly seek a solution which may take weeks, months, or even years. Your response changes in the face of suffering and problems. That is important, for you do not determine the hardships of your life or how long you suffer. Some people suffer all their lives. Love is patient—even while a person is suffering.

LOVE IS KIND

The speaker was a highly educated, well-respected man. He had been married twenty years.

His wife had a firm, unshakable conviction that it was the duty and responsibility of the man of the house to take out the garbage. So, every morning after he kissed her goodbye, she would hand him a bag or two of garbage. His normal routine was to grab the bags, stomp out of the house, and slam the garbage into the can.

"That takes care of your old garbage," he would mutter to no one as he got into his car and squealed around the corner. This was a twenty-year battle.

Then he discovered the love of God, and that love is always kind. It startled him to realize what an unkind act he was performing every morning. He still carries out the garbage. It is still a concession, but it is done now with a kindly spirit toward his wife.

He discovered further that he carried out many of his other daily duties with the same unkindly spirit. He realized he was the architect of his own misery. This man let the love of God bathe his miserable spirit. Without changing a single detail in his life, he began enjoying the jobs instead of seeing them as distasteful chores.

A corporation I worked for was civic-minded and pressured its employees to give a day's pay to the annual United Fund drive. There was much griping and complaining, but most employees fell in step. Some made a contribution with a kindly spirit, some under much protest. In either case, you wrote a check. It is the spirit, not the deed, that demonstrates kindness.

We are all called upon to do things we would rather not do. To do them with an unkindly spirit is to create our own suffering. If kindness is an act of love, then you can express kindness to your wife, my wife, all men and women. Serving a glass of water, carrying a bag of groceries, or holding a door open may or may not be an act of love.

Love is not saying certain words or behaving in a certain way. Love is evidenced by your inner reaction to strangers as well as to the people who are close and intimate with you. The love of God in you will determine whether your outer behavior toward your mother, father, wife, children, in-laws, relatives, neighbors, friends, and coworkers is an act of love. Love is kind.

LOVE IS NOT JEALOUS

Jealousy can result in terrible personal suffering. I refer to discontent, ill will, resentment, spite, unhappiness, or mental uneasiness toward someone else's success, superiority, or advantage. It can involve animosity toward a rival or suspected infidelity.

Jean and Martha were college pals. Jean fell for the school's star athlete and married him, only to discover he was an average person apart from his athletic ability. Now, Jean and her husband live in a tiny house and barely make ends meet on her husband's low salary. He happily spends evenings playing on neighborhood teams. The spectators love him.

Martha married a bookworm. Jean could not stand him, but the bookworm ended up doing well in the business world. Martha lives in a big, beautiful home, wears elegant clothes, drives a big car, and moves in professional circles.

Jean burns with jealousy over her husband's popularity and Martha's comfortable life. This is the opposite of admiration and happiness toward a person.

Malcolm has a knack for making profitable land deals which his wife, Helen, cannot understand. If he followed her advice, he would never get involved because she is sure he is making a mistake. His judgment bothers her, even though she benefits. This is another type of jealousy.

The love of God is the opposite of jealousy. His love would help Jean and Helen to appreciate the talent, ability, and opportunities of other people.

Love is not jealous.

LOVE IS NOT BOASTFUL OR PROUD

Carl came to see me for two reasons. His wife disliked him, and he was having trouble keeping friends. After that introduction, he went ahead and chronicled his success in the insurance business. Then he told me about his college athletic career. His name was a household word, and autograph seekers made him the center of attention.

At this moment, Carl's wife cut in.

"I've heard that same speech hundreds of times."

I soon realized that Carl's conversations were one-sided. He did not listen to other people; he just waited for them to pause so he could resume bragging.

According to his wife, his business success was just average among their friends. They could not care less about his college career. To them, he was just an arrogant person. She was right. Carl demanded consideration not due him and was self-assertive beyond the bounds of modesty.

GOD'S LOVE DOES NOT . . .

I was a speaker recently at a family camp. We had a leader named Don who had the ability to set a group of strangers at ease quickly. He remembered names. Before you knew it, you were singing energetically and getting acquainted. He used his talents to bless others instead of to impress—the opposite of bragging and pride.

The love of God does not brag. It is not proud.

- **Love does not act haughty.**
- **Love does not seek its own.**
- **Love is not rude.**
- **Love is not irritable or touchy.**

These characteristics of love can be combined: love does not act unbecomingly, for it does not seek its own and, therefore, is not easily provoked.

Sometimes, however, there are surprises in store for you. To your amazement, you are saying and doing things that hardly fit these three elements of the love of God.

As a speaker, I am often away from home. When our children were small, we had an ironclad rule: I would never be away for a full week. Once, when 2,000 miles away from home, two days of my tour were canceled. My next commitment was 500 miles away. What to do? Stick around or go home?

"I'll do it. I'll go home and surprise them." So I did. Two thousand miles. And after flying all night long, I arrived home about 8:30 A.M.

My wife was just leaving. It was a letdown, but, after all, she had her plans. And I had not called her. My arrival was to be a surprise. So we agreed to meet at home in a few hours. I went to the basement and filled in the time puttering around until she returned. I heard the car pull into the driveway and began anticipating.

"She'll come right down. I know it," I said to myself. She came in, but she went directly—upstairs. So I banged a hammer a couple of times to make sure she would know where I was. "Now she'll come for sure." I could see it. My wife would come down to the basement, fall into my arms, and tell me how good it was to have me home.

But she did not. I decided not to budge. After all, I had traveled all that distance just to be with her and the kids. You would think she would come down and tell me how good it was for me to be home! But she didn't.

I was really mad. Mind you, less than twenty-four hours earlier, I had been teaching people how to walk in the spirit of love—how to be patient and long-suffering. Finally, I stomped upstairs. She was getting lunch ready and gave me a cold shoulder.

If she doesn't want to talk to me, I'm certainly not going to talk to her. I was huffing and puffing inside.

We sat down to a miserable lunch. I glared at her. She glared at me. Finally, I got up from the table and went into the living room, feeling that certainly she would come in and sit down with me. She started up the sewing machine! And there I sat, a smoldering keg of temperamental dynamite, finally blurting, "Will you shut off that sewing machine? I traveled clear across the country to come home and you don't pay attention to me!"

"What do you mean?" she snapped back.

"Well, I'm home, and you're sewing!"

"Did you just get home?" She was blazing now. "Why didn't you come up to see me? You didn't have to stay in the basement!"

How about that? I was downstairs simmering. She was upstairs simmering. I was thinking that the least she could do was come down and see me. She was thinking, "If he can fly 2,000 miles to see me, then how come he can't walk up the stairs?"

Can you believe it? Two grown-up people acting like that? God's love was missing. Love does not act unbecoming, for it does not seek its own and, therefore, is not rude, irritable, or touchy. We really flunked that test.

What do justified people do when they realize they are wrong? The Bible tells us:

> **But if we walk in the light as He is in the light, we**
> **have fellowship with one another, and the blood**
> **of Jesus Christ His Son cleanses us from all sin.**
> 1 JOHN 1:7

The foolishness of our behavior hit both of us like a light, and we confessed our sins (unbecoming self-seeking, rude, irritable, or touchy behavior) to God and let Him bathe our hearts once again with His love. Our fellowship was restored.

The love of God turns you into a person who is watchful, careful, and sensitive to the people around you. Without it, you turn back to self-seeking.

- **Love does not act unbecoming, does not seek its own, is not rude, irritable, or touchy.**
- **Love will hardly even notice when others do wrong.**
- **Love does not hold grudges.**
- **Love does not rejoice in injustices.**

There are some common "wrongs" that occur over and over. We are all familiar with the following:

- A husband doesn't allow enough time for his wife and friends.
- A wife neglects her husband and family.
- One partner is financially irresponsible.
- There is emotional or physical involvement with someone else.
- One partner indulges or pampers the children.

The offended partner retaliates.

There is a real "wrong" involved—no doubt about it. The sad part is that the wronged person often ends up in the consulting room, angry, bitter, and resentful.

"Why not?" is the normal question fired at me.

There is a better way. Respond with God's love (patient, longsuffering, kind). You still have the problem, but you work on it without suffering. Remember that anger, resentment, and bitterness in the wronged person do not necessarily bother the one who is wrong.

To know that God's love is available to you when you need it the most is wonderful—for example, when you are wronged.

The other side of the coin would be to rejoice when others are wrong. Perhaps your partner has lectured you on your unacceptable behavior and now is doing the same thing. You may be glad.

Someone else's children are in trouble, and you are happy. You deliberately come home late and smugly enjoy it when your partner loses his or her temper.

The love of God in you does not stop because of a wrong suffered. Nor do you enjoy seeing someone else doing wrong or enjoy retaliating wrongly yourself. Love does not take into account wrong suffered, does not rejoice in unrighteousness.

A woman speaks of being neglected by her husband. He refuses to share in the rearing of the children, to go to church with her, or to supply adequate furniture for the house; he spends many nights away from home. In return, she refuses to cook breakfast for him, to visit his relatives, or to entertain his friends. During counseling he agreed that all she said about him was true, but if she would not meet him partway in some of these differences, he would continue treating her as he had been doing.

The wife insisted that it was up to him to make the first move. If this is true, then how could we ever pass on to others the love of Christ?

A hurtful relationship develops when two people violate the principles of Christian living. Paul says,

> **Repay no one evil for evil. Have regard for good
> things in the sight of all men. If it is possible, as
> much as depends on you, live peaceably with all
> men. Beloved, do not avenge yourselves, but
> *rather* give place to wrath; for it is written,
> "*Vengeance is Mine, I will repay,*" says the Lord.**
> ROMANS 12:17–19

Another woman tells of her life with her husband. He came home drunk night after night. At times he would beat her. They quarreled constantly over the training of their children. They quarreled over the use of the car. They quarreled over how to spend the money, over the type of entertainment, over religion. In a moment of remorse, he would buy her jewelry and clothing as a peace offering, but, in her anger, she would refuse to wear these things.

Over a period of time, this woman saw her need of the Savior. She needed God's strength if she was to have the attitude of Jesus. She looked to God for strength to react as she should toward her husband. She ceased resisting him and did everything she could to please him. Soon she discovered that she enjoyed trying to please him and that she did it because she wanted to do it. Her husband's behavior has not changed. She is not treating him well in order to change him. *She is reacting kindly toward her husband because she submits to the love of God through faith in Christ.* This is not to say that she does not want her husband to change his ways. He has stopped hitting her.

LOVE REJOICES WITH THE TRUTH

Every morning you wake up with some facts to face. These include memories of yesterday, the demands of today, and the unknowns of tomorrow. Look at some of the facts:

Married or unmarried	Pretty or not pretty
Children or no children	Educated or uneducated
Alone or with someone	Rich or poor
Strong or weak	Employed or unemployed
Tall or short	Treated well or mistreated
Sick or well	

Before you get out of bed, you can let the love of God bathe your heart. Then you can rejoice in these truths (and others)—bear all things, believe all things, hope all things, endure all things—without taking into account wrongs suffered or contemplating unrighteous choices.

You can accept yourself, the positives and negatives.

Everyone faces a set of daily truths. You have yours, and I have mine. God's love helps us to accept unchangeable circumstances and helps us to enjoy working on them.

SPEAKING THE TRUTH

There is another kind of truth, involving the thoughts, opinions, and behavior of other people.

"I wouldn't dare give all my opinions or reveal all my thoughts," says one of my clients. "My partner would be upset, feel hurt, hold a grudge, or would never forgive me."

How true. Communication often is cut off when one partner does not like the other's opinion. One partner must face the truth about his wife's housekeeping and her reactions to his opinions. She must face his opinions about her choices and his subsequent reaction. Neither likes the truth because the truth exposes deception, hatred, resentment, rebellion, self-centeredness, or impatience in the other partner.

Healthy marriages are built on the cornerstone of rejoicing in the truth. You enjoy hearing what your partner is thinking. It gives you a realistic picture of your relationship.

Love rejoices with the truth.

LOVE IS LOYAL NO MATTER WHAT THE COST (LOVE BEARS ALL THINGS)

As you face life's difficulties, God's love helps you bear heartaches, pain, bruises, suffering, and problems without spilling over on other people. You do not have to spill everything out right now—if you are really loving.

We all have problems, but *God's love makes either a gentleman or a lady out of us.* You can bear your own burdens without spilling on others who are uninterested or cannot help. Free from envy and strife, you can think straight. Now, tackling problems can be a pleasure.

With this attitude, you accept the best in people as long as possible.

Bill and Karen married a few days after they graduated from high school. His job as a supermarket stock boy paid very little, but they loved each other.

"That's what counts," they agreed. They were soon deep in debt. Then, the other shoe fell. Bill was fired for loafing.

The next ten years were a succession of rough experiences. Bill enrolled in college, and Karen went to work. Halfway through the semester, he quit. He lost a succession of jobs: truck driver, tool shop worker, vacuum cleaner salesman, and insurance salesman.

Two children were born. As soon as possible Karen was back at work. Bill, however, loafed around the house, causing their families and friends to write him off.

Karen had days when she was ready to leave, but she found Jesus and His love. She wavered at times but always repented and asked God to restore her belief in her husband and renew her patience. Meanwhile she encouraged, urged, and pressured Bill.

Finally, Bill was working as a fry cook, night shift. That's about all you can expect of him, everyone thought. Things were different this time. Like a butterfly, Bill emerged from his cocoon.

In quick succession, he was on days, then in charge of the kitchen, then in charge of training cooks for this restaurant chain, then in charge of food management for the chain, then owning his own restaurant. Today, Bill is a respected, prosperous businessman.

It was a long, long road for Karen. But God's love had sustained her. Love believes all things—even for ten years.

"You can't trust anyone," Jerome growled at me, basing his judgment on two traumatic incidents. Several years ago his wife ran off with one of his friends. A dozen years ago, another "friend" skipped town and left him to pay off a note Jerome had cosigned.

When I told him that God's love could restore his belief in people, Jerome exploded with rage and stomped out of the consulting room to nurse his grudges. Of course, he was seriously wronged, but his rage did not bother the people who wronged him. They never even knew where he was. He was the architect of his own suffering.

To be sure, there are untrustworthy people. After you have done everything possible to establish a person's integrity and they still mislead, God's love will sustain your faith in other people.

Harold risked all he had in a business venture against the resistance of his wife. It was going beautifully until the economy dipped. Instead of having rosy prospects, Harold was deeply in debt and without an income. He faced a wife who told him so and some unhappy investors. He could turn on himself, bemoan his situation, and berate himself. The others could do the same. They all needed the love of God toward one another, or they could wallow in self-pity.

"No one cares about me, especially God," and "That's what I get for believing in free enterprise," he said.

Or they could hasten back to God and let Him renew their spirits. Harold chose to turn to God. What a change in his thoughts!

"I may be bankrupt, and that's bad. But I'm not sick, and that's good.

I am bankrupt and unemployed. That's double bad. Regardless, I still have a family, and that's good. I have an education and some ability. That's double good."

With his hope in God renewed, Harold tackled his problems. Nothing changed with the snap of two fingers. Creditors hounded him unmercifully. Two years later, he was back on the track. Now he has a good job and is slowly repaying his creditors. Sustained by hope in God, he's experienced something that ruined other men.

There was no easy way out. But no matter what people said or what he heard, Harold's hope spurred him on. He almost crossed himself off, but God's love carried him through the trial.

His wife and the investors followed Harold's example. They learned that the love of God gave them the strength they needed to ride out a business disaster.

It was Jesus who said,

"These things I have spoken to you, that in Me you may have peace. In the world you will have tribulation; but be of good cheer, I have overcome the world."
JOHN 16:33

We cringe in the face of financial crisis, sickness, mistreatment, mis-understandings, rejection, and persecution. Our inner response is the problem. Self-seeking and the deeds of the flesh cause suffering.

However, the person who looks forward to each day with a zest for living understands that life involves facing one problem after another. Part of the fun of living is to look forward to the next problem and the challenge of working it out with the love of God in your heart.

This is a good time to review the elements of God's love:

• Love is patient and kind.
• Love is never jealous or envious.
• Love is never boastful or proud.

- Love is never haughty or selfish or rude.
- Love does not demand its own way.
- Love is not irritable or touchy.
- Love does not hold grudges.
- Love will hardly even notice when others do it wrong.
- Love is never glad about injustice.
- Love rejoices when truth wins out.
- Love is loyal no matter what the cost, always believes in others.
- Love expects the best of others.
- Love stands its ground in defending others (1 Cor. 13:4–7, adapted from LB).

Since God is the source, this love can be universally applied. It is spiritual fruit. It is to know no limits. It is broader than the union of two people in a marriage. Thus, it cannot be love that sets one man and woman apart as the two that shall become one flesh.

If it is not love that produces the uniqueness of marriage, what is it? It is the relationship—a commitment of the duties and details of marriage—that sets a man and a woman apart.

You are to love all men. The relationship that binds you and your mate together is exclusively yours.

All of us are involved in a number of relationships. Some unite us with fellow workers in a job, with neighbors in a community undertaking, with other Christians in the conduct of a local church program. Each relationship has its own peculiarities, its own limits. Marriage is the most sacred and intimate of all relationships. But if love is a universal thing, marriage has no monopoly on it.

To yield to the love of God is to produce a perfect love toward others, including the marriage partner. Conversely, faulty relationships are the result of a faulty relationship with God. A marriage based on sincere love for God can be disturbed only when personal sin comes between one or the other of the individuals and God.

The relationship of marriage, however, is no guarantor of happiness. A husband and wife may live under the same roof, spend each other's money, sleep in the same room, eat together, give birth to children from a shared physical experience. But without the undergirding of the love of God, the intimacies of the marriage relationship can drive a couple apart.

The trivialities of housekeeping nearly sent Peter and Sally into divorce court. She made the bed only when it was time to get into it again, seldom dusted, and was a miserable housekeeper. He never was around when she needed help and let the car go to ruin for lack of care. Petty quarrels grew to bitterness. When seen against the elements of God's love, their marriage surely did not measure up. Each came to realize, however, just where their smoldering resentments were leading, and in repentance for their rebellion against God as much as each other, both sought the love they lacked. Only then did they discover that prayerful, congenial discussion could lead to solutions of their problems.

Circumstances in a marriage change. Feelings do not remain the same. Physical responses vary from day to day. The thousandth kiss does not hold the thrill of the first kiss. Passion tapers off. If it did not, you could not stand the pace.

Because the old thrill is no longer there, a couple will sometimes ask, "Is our marriage doomed?" An individual will wonder, "Was I mistaken in my choice of a partner?"

You cannot expect today's reactions to be carbon copies of those you experienced when your marriage began ten or twenty years ago. You have changed. So has your mate. So have the conditions surrounding your marriage. But you learn to take these changes in stride because God's love provides the patience, kindness, unselfishness, and sincerity to cope with them.

"For better, for worse," the marriage vow reads. The relationship may lead toward either pole. The couple walking together in God's love will endure.

WHEN YOU NEED LOVE THE MOST!

God's love can bind you together. Review the list of elements. Memorize them. They will restore the thrill of hugging and kissing, the warmth of friendship.

When do you need the love of God the most? Usually, when you shun it—during the problem, while the discussion is going on, when you are being ignored, or if the decision goes against you.

Couples in trouble need the love of God and the grace of God. They still face the same problems. The love of God eliminates the friction, allowing them to resolve their differences.

Your negative response results from the absence of God's love, not from the presence or choices of your partner.

> **And may the Lord make you increase and abound in**
> **love to one another and to all, just as we *do* to you.**
> 1 Thessalonians 3:12

A New Option

What do you do when you are not drawing upon the love of God? You admit your mistake, then recall God's promise in Romans 5:5:

> **Now hope does not disappoint, because the love**
> **of God has been poured out in our hearts by the**
> **Holy Spirit who was given to us.**

Then you ask Him to restore that missing element of God's love. You let God give you His love when you need it. The choice is yours.

Try it.

Let God bathe your heart with His kind of love (recheck the list). Then you will get on with making your marriage better—God's way!

CHAPTER 4

Steps to Spiritual Strength

. . . but present yourselves to God . . .
ROMANS 6:13B

There are some steps that will enable you to establish a marriage God's way. These steps are as follows:

1. Evaluate your behavior.
2. Accept your condition.
3. Receive forgiveness from God.
4. Surrender to the power of God for cleansing and the fruit of the Spirit.

Taking this series of steps will bring your life into continuous subjection to the will of God, who wants you to love your neighbor as yourself. If you do not know Jesus Christ as your Savior, consider seeking someone out today who can show you how to know Him personally.

EVALUATE YOUR BEHAVIOR

Before you can solve a problem, you must first find out what the problem is. This is an orderly world. It operates according to definite, dependable laws.

For example, we take care to make allowance for the law of gravity. A dear, elderly gentleman put up a ladder to do some work on his roof, but he placed it so that it was crooked. When he climbed up the ladder, it began to slide. He fell and broke his hip. Here was a man, a devout Christian, who was careless about observing the law of gravity. He fell just as the worst criminal would have fallen if he had gone up the ladder.

People take the laws of friction into account. A student took a curve in the road too fast on an icy day. His car went end over end, and he came out of the wreckage with a battered head. He had ignored the laws of friction. He did not do this intentionally. He was not deliberately reckless, yet the same thing happened to him as would have happened to the most reckless of drivers.

All of us know the importance of abiding by the laws of gravity and friction. These laws have been gathered together in books. As we study them, we learn what to expect if we abide by them and what to expect if we violate them.

The laws of human behavior are likewise gathered together in a Book—the Bible. To understand why people behave as they do and to understand why you behave as you do, you must understand the laws contained in the Bible. The apostle says of the Bible:

> **All Scripture *is* given by inspiration of God, and *is* profitable for doctrine, for reproof, for correction, for instruction in righteousness, that the man of God may be complete, thoroughly equipped for every good work.**
> 2 TIMOTHY 3:16–17

The cause of inner unrest, conflict between people, and separation from God is the violation of the laws found in the Bible.

Behold, the LORD's hand is not shortened
That it cannot save;
Nor His ear heavy,
That it cannot hear.
But your iniquities have separated you from your God;
And your sins have hidden *His* face from you,
So that He will not hear.

ISAIAH 59:1–2

Whether done deliberately or in ignorance, we reap the results of violating God's laws, just as we reap the result of violating the laws of friction or gravity.

To understand the cause of inner unrest, conflict with people, and separation from God is to understand the effect of sin. To understand God's solution is to understand the preventatives that keep us from sinning.

OUR TENDENCY TO SIN

The tendency to sin is described by Paul and put into modern English by Charles B. Williams:

> "Indeed, I do not understand what I do, for I do not practice what I want to do, but I am always doing what I hate. But if I am always doing what I do not want to do, I agree that the law is right. Now really it is not I that am doing these things, but it is sin which has its home within me. For I know that nothing good has its home in me; that is, in my lower self; I have the will but not the power to do what is right. Indeed, I do not do the good things that I want to do, but I do practice the evil things that I do not want to do. But if I do the things that I do not want to do, it is really not I that am doing these

things, but it is sin which has its home within me. So I find this law: When I want to do right, the wrong is always in my way. For in accordance with my better inner nature I approve God's law, but I see another power operating in my lower nature in conflict with the power operated by my reason, which makes me a prisoner to the power of sin which is operating in my lower nature."

ROMANS 7:15–23

To illustrate, a student tells of his experience. Night after night, before he retired, he determined that he would go through the next day with a wholesome, positive reaction toward circumstances and people. One morning he was particularly determined to have a good day. He left his room, raced for the elevator, and just as he got there the door closed. He was forced to wait a few minutes. When he did get on the elevator, another passenger accidentally stepped on his foot. He walked away very conscious of being annoyed at both incidents in spite of his determination to react in a wholesome, kindly way toward all such happenings.

Again, a mother of two preschool children tells of her struggle with her attitude toward her children. Two specific tasks that faced her daily caused her much annoyance. She hated herself for it, but no amount of determination, willpower, or good intentions could give her control over her annoyance at feeding picky children or dealing with their fusses. Granted, these are trying tasks. The point is that this woman was unable to achieve the desired attitude toward these tasks.

All of us sooner or later find ourselves doing, saying, feeling, thinking in a way that is distasteful to us. All of us, sooner or later, find ourselves not doing, saying, or feeling as we would like. This tendency is sin—something within you that is beyond your control. To recognize and accept this tendency within you is the first step toward a solution to the problem.

SPECIFIC ACTS THAT ARE SIN

The tendency within you makes itself known to you by specific inner reactions or outward action toward others.

Anger, bitterness, wrath, pride, and hate are inner reactions to circumstances. These are invisible and can be concealed. Any man who will compare himself with the Bible's standard must declare himself a sinner, unable to eliminate from his life the inward reactions or outward responses undesirable to him and described in God's Word as sin.

We tend to overemphasize the value and importance of outward behavior and to minimize—or fail to realize—the importance given in the Bible to inward behavior. It is impossible for another to see within you, and you are prone to hide even from yourself. James says,

> **But if you have bitter envy and self-seeking in**
> **your hearts, do not boast and lie against the truth.**
> **This wisdom does not descend from above, but** *is*
> **earthly, sensual, demonic.**
> JAMES 3:14–15

THE LAW OF LIFE IN CHRIST JESUS

To bring into sharper focus the meaning of sin and its terrible result to you, you should consider another important law:

> **For the law of the Spirit of life in Christ Jesus has**
> **made me free from the law of sin and death.**
> ROMANS 8:2

> **But the fruit of the Spirit is love, joy, peace, long-**
> **suffering, kindness, goodness, faithfulness, gentle-**
> **ness, self-control. Against such there is no law.**
> GALATIANS 5:22–23

Again, these are inward, invisible qualities. You can act this way in your own strength, at least part of the time; but you can't genuinely be this way without the power of the indwelling Holy Spirit. If you doubt it, just pay attention to your inner responses to people or circumstances for one week.

ACCEPT YOUR CONDITION

It is easy and common to find a reason outside of yourself that keeps you from loving your neighbor as yourself. It seems reasonable that missing an elevator, getting a toe stepped on, feeding picky children and dealing with their fusses, living with a mother who can't understand, associating with people who have undesirable habits, and living with an uncooperative wife or husband are justifiable reasons for being disturbed. Under such circumstances anger, wrath, malice, bitterness, resentment, and the like seem normal.

This reasoning seems to be sound. However, the Bible calls such reactions sinful. In other words, these circumstances are not putting these reactions into you; they are bringing these reactions out of you.

> So Jesus said, "Are you also still without under-
> standing? Do you not yet understand that what-
> ever enters the mouth goes into the stomach and is
> eliminated? But those things which proceed out of
> the mouth come from the heart, and they defile a
> man. For out of the heart proceed evil thoughts,
> murders, adulteries, fornications, thefts, false wit-
> ness, blasphemies."
> MATTHEW 15:16–19

Many people find this to be a shocking idea. It seems clear that the circumstances or the other person is the cause of their distress. It is hard to realize that distress is a response to the circumstance or person.

The answer is that you can find peace and contentment without changing your circumstances or the people in your life. To do so involves recognizing that the situation you are in is not causing your distress. You must accept or acknowledge personal responsibility for your distress, for your sin.

> "*There is* no peace,"
> Says my God, "for the wicked."
> ISAIAH 57:21

> Behold, the LORD's hand is not shortened,
> That it cannot save;
> Nor His ear heavy,
> That it cannot hear.
> But your iniquities have separated you from your God;
> And your sins have hidden *His* face from you,
> So that He will not hear.
> ISAIAH 59:1–2

You need a power outside yourself if you are to respond differently the next time you find yourself in your trying circumstance. You must accept personal responsibility without reservation. Dependence and faith in willpower, resolutions, insight, and determination are not the answer. A lingering thought that another person must be at least a little bit to blame is not the answer.

It is amazing how many people prefer to find a reason for justifying anger, wrath, malice, envy, and similar emotions rather than finding freedom from them. People prefer to change the circumstance or the person rather than to seek a source of peace, joy, and comfort in the circumstance or with the person.

For example, consider a young man who had habits that his mother believed were bad. The mother kept insisting that her misery was caused by her son's behavior. Accordingly, this mother felt quite clear in her own mind that the solution to her problem was to see a change in her son. Further, this woman believed that, being a Christian, she should not be agreeable toward her son, lest she seem to be giving her blessing upon her son's unacceptable habits. She was being a good Christian, she thought, by being angry and impatient with her son. The son, in turn, felt quite justified in being bitter, rebellious, hostile, and stubborn. He would not give in if it killed him. If there was a source of strength that would enable him to have a spirit of love, tenderness, gentleness, and compassion toward his mother, he would turn away from it. He insisted that his mother was the cause of these reactions.

The woman who had the task of teaching two small children how to eat right and how to get along preferred to be annoyed. According to her, you should be annoyed at such a job. There is nothing wrong with being impatient with such a task. It is quite normal to be disgusted, tense, and dissatisfied at the end of the day. The children are the cause of these reactions. In her opinion, being a Christian has no bearing on the matter.

Many Christians find comfort in speaking of nerves, tension, anxiety, or stress—any term but sin. Many Christians feel that they have long ago settled the matter of living in sin. They are saved. They are sanctified. But remember our definition of sin!

> **Whoever commits sin also commits lawlessness,**
> **and sin is lawlessness.**
> 1 JOHN 3:4

If it applies, then it applies. It matters not who you are, how much responsibility you have, what your status is, or who your family is. You may have been trained to believe that to grin and bear it, even though you are seething inside, is evidence of piety; to speak in a well-modulated voice, even though you feel like screaming, is a mark of culture; to perform the task assigned, even though you rebel inwardly, is evidence of determination. Such behavior is surely to be expected from a social standpoint. However, from a personal standpoint you benefit nothing. Your inward reaction is evidence of sinfulness. Jesus warned the Pharisees:

"Now you Pharisees make the outside of the cup
and dish clean, but your inward part is full of
greed and wickedness. Foolish ones! Did not He
who made the outside make the inside also?"
LUKE 11:39–40

You have seen that acceptance of your condition implies accepting personal responsibility without reservation. If you feel that you can and will conquer your circumstances, then you are not yet ready to accept the tendency to sin. It is best for you to try yourself. Expose yourself to your circumstances and pay attention to your inner reactions and your outward actions. Acceptance means that you are convinced beyond the shadow of a doubt that you are subject to your tendency to sin and that this causes you to react the way you do not want to react—and prevents you from reacting in a way that you would like to react. This applies to thoughts, feelings, desires, actions, or speech. These must be identified in detail and dealt with separately. Acceptance or acknowledgment of the presence of sin in your life opens the way for you to avail yourself of a better way of life as defined by Paul:

For the law of the Spirit of life in Christ Jesus has
made me free from the law of sin and death.
ROMANS 8:2

RECEIVE FORGIVENESS FROM GOD

Christ died to make forgiveness available to us:

In Him we have redemption through His blood,
the forgiveness of sins, according to the riches of
His grace.
EPHESIANS 1:7

Thus far you have seen that acceptance of your tendency to sin is often a difficult step to take. Seeking forgiveness is a more difficult step to take. At first glance, this step seems easy. In practice, the sinful nature is a useful tool and not easily laid down. To illustrate, a wife is fearful that if she does not display jealousy, she will lose control over her husband's affection. A mother is fearful that if she does not threaten to be angry with her children, she will lose control over their behavior. A young man does not want to give up the pleasure of lusting after women. A girl feels that to cease her rebellion against her parents is evidence of weakness. To acknowledge these reactions as sin is a step that is very difficult for many people to take. To seek forgiveness for sins is harder yet. To ask for forgiveness implies repentance and a willingness to forsake sins.

> **He who covers his sins will not prosper,**
> **But whoever confesses and forsakes *them* will**
> **have mercy.**
> PROVERBS 28:13

> **Let the wicked forsake his way,**
> **And the unrighteous man his thoughts;**
> **Let him return to the LORD,**
> **And He will have mercy on him;**
> **And to our God,**
> **For He will abundantly pardon.**
> ISAIAH 55:7

Many people insist that a period of depression, self-condemnation, sadness, remorse, or weeping is evidence of repentance. In Quebec, one can see people climb five hundred cathedral steps on their knees in evidence of repentance. In India, a man may be lying on a bed of spikes. It is true that conviction of sin causes some people to react emotionally or to show evidence of repentance. However, repentance is not the emotion or the action. It is, rather, being sorry enough for sin to hate and forsake it. Repentance involves following God's plan and believing His Word:

If we confess our sins, He is faithful and just to forgive us *our* sins and to cleanse us from all unrighteousness.
1 JOHN 1:9

The simplicity of receiving forgiveness is hard to accept. It does seem that we ought to help God out somehow. Nothing is required of you apart from acceptance of your sinfulness and of God's forgiveness on His terms, not yours. To repeat, this must be done from the heart. There is no other way. You must be completely sincere. You will not find forgiveness until you are convinced that you need it, that you are undone, that there is no other way.

Yes, acceptance of your tendency to sin, confession of specific sins, and seeking forgiveness are contrary to our normal way of doing things. But the next step—surrender to the power of God—is the hardest of all to accept.

SURRENDER TO THE POWER OF GOD

At first glance, it would seem that to submit to the strength and power of God is something that everyone would gladly do. As Paul expresses it,

Not that we are sufficient of ourselves to think of anything as *being* from ourselves, but our sufficiency *is* from God.
2 CORINTHIANS 3:5

On the contrary, man rebels against accepting his weakness or insufficiency. However, even if you acknowledge failures of the past, you will not necessarily acknowledge your inability to please God in the future. Man tends to feel that since he understands the reason for past failures, he can now do better. He tends to seek the answer to his sinfulness in two ways: to repent for past sins and to retain confidence in himself not to repeat past sins. He tends to retain his faith in his own self-discipline, willpower, training, self-sacrifice, and the like.

To surrender to God implies a lifetime study of His will for every detail of your life. It means recognizing your inability to do His will apart from His power and your need to submit to Him daily for His power. To quote Paul further:

> For it is the God who commanded light to shine out of darkness who has shone in our hearts to *give* the light of the knowledge of the glory of God in the face of Jesus Christ. But we have this treasure in earthen vessels, that the excellence of the power may be of God and not of us. *We are* hard pressed on every side, yet not crushed; *we are* perplexed, but not in despair; persecuted, but not forsaken; struck down, but not destroyed—always carrying about in the body the dying of the Lord Jesus, that the life of Jesus also may be manifested in our body.
>
> 2 CORINTHIANS 4:6–10

Note three basic truths in these verses: Christ is the treasure, the earthen vessels are our bodies, and the all-surpassing power is of God and not of us. Therefore, this treasure is from God, and we experience the power of God in our lives as we recognize its source and submit to Him who gives it.

Yes, the power to please God comes from God. Paul says of the Lord Jesus:

> But of Him you are in Christ Jesus, who became for us wisdom from God—and righteousness and

sanctification and redemption—that, as it is written, "He who glories, let him glory in the LORD."
1 CORINTHIANS 1:30–31

The apostle's prayer for the Colossians was

that you may walk worthy of the Lord, fully
pleasing *Him,* being fruitful in every good work
and increasing in the knowledge of God;
strengthened with all might, according to His glorious power, for all patience and longsuffering
with joy.
COLOSSIANS 1:10–11

Note Romans 15:13; Isaiah 26:3; 32:17; Philippians 3:9;
1 Corinthians 1:2–7.

Again, turning to Williams' translation of Romans 7:24–8:4, we
read:

Wretched man that I am! Who can save me from this
deadly lower nature? Thank God! it has been done
through Jesus Christ our Lord! . . . So then there is no
condemnation at all for those who are in union with
Christ Jesus. For the life-giving power of the Spirit
through union with Christ Jesus has set us free from the
power of sin and death. For though the law could not do
it, because it was made helpless through our lower
nature, yet God, by sending His own Son in a body similar to that of our lower nature, and as a sacrifice for sin,
passed sentence upon sin through His body, so that the
requirement of the law might be fully met in us who do
not live by the standard set by our lower nature, but by
the standard set by the Spirit.

To surrender to God involves both a crisis and a daily process. There needs to be a clear, definite yielding of one's self completely to God, followed by day-by-day experience of that surrender. Note Paul's words in Romans 6:13:

> **And do not present your members *as* instruments**
> **of unrighteousness to sin, but present yourselves to**
> **God as being alive from the dead, and your mem-**
> **bers *as* instruments of righteousness to God.**
> ROMANS 6:13

And again, in Romans 12:1–2:

> **. . . that you present your bodies a living sacrifice . . .**
> **but be transformed by the renewing of your mind . . .**
> ROMANS 12:1B–2

What do these passages mean? Simply this: that we are to give ourselves—body, mind, and soul—unreservedly to God. This is a matter of the will. Are you willing? Then how is this to be accomplished?

Again, the Word of God is clear about this matter. It is by the work of the Holy Spirit. We must not only thank God for the indwelling of the Holy Spirit in our hearts (John 14:16–17; Rom. 8:9), but we must heed the command of the Word that we are to

> **be filled with the Spirit.**
> EPHESIANS 5:18B

Here is the secret of God's power—the Holy Spirit expressing Himself through us! He works in us only as we let Him. This is the very reason that Paul said,

> **. . . but present yourselves to God . . .**
> ROMANS 6:13B

A young woman was married to a man who refused to give her spending money. This disturbed her to the extent that she was always feeling sorry for herself and angry with her husband. She went to an older woman in the church who was known to be a calm, peaceful soul. The older woman said to the younger one, "Let me tell you my story. My husband keeps all the money. He seldom pays any attention to my opinion. Now that the children are married, he gives most of his time to them and has no room for me in his life. This has gone on for thirty years. It will probably go on as long as I live. All these years I have prayed daily for patience and every day God answers my prayer."

Take another look at the phrase "I pray daily for patience." Is patience not a fruit of the Spirit? Is patience not available automatically? Perhaps a daily routine will clarify the process. When I wake up in a dark room, I turn on a light and the darkness disappears. It is a fantastic miracle that I perform without thinking. Light is at my fingertips, but it does not come on automatically. I must turn it on. If the room is cold, it requires a different process to warm it up that is unrelated to light.

If you wake up and you are impatient, you let God replace it with patience. I do not know how it works. It is a miracle. You must still deal with an indifferent husband, which is a totally different problem than needing patience.

Yes, to surrender to God is to bring each circumstance of life to Him and receive from Him the strength to face it by His Spirit. It is one thing to make a broad, thoughtless statement that you will submit to God and another thing to surrender each detail of life to Him.

When you are impatient, you lack patience; when you are unhappy, you lack joy; when you are tense and anxious, you lack peace. You must continuously go to the source of supply. Comfort, mercy, grace, peace, joy, patience, and longsuffering with joyfulness will be yours only when you recognize that you lack them and when you let God give them to you.

Just as you need your food and water supply daily, so also you need your supply of joy, peace, and other spiritual qualities daily. Read Psalm 103:5 and 1 Corinthians 4:16.

**Who satisfies your mouth with good *things*,
So *that* your youth is renewed like the eagle's.**
PSALM 103:5

Therefore I urge you, imitate me.
1 CORINTHIANS 4:16

Ten years from now you will still draw your strength and power from God just as you will need to eat food and drink water. To understand this and to act accordingly is the key to a life that will enable you to love your neighbor as yourself and to do it consistently.

CHAPTER 5

Maintaining Good Marital Communication

The secret of good fellowship in marriage lies in two people applying the principle embodied in this verse:

> **"And just as you want men to do to you, you also do to them likewise."**
> LUKE 6:31

Here is a workable formula, and, amazingly, it is easier to carry out than to try to figure out the other person and treat him accordingly.

Scott and Ann found this out. Like practically everyone, each longed to be appreciated and have their viewpoint respected. They discovered that the rule Jesus gave is just as effective today as when He spoke it.

Scott sought counsel because he was puzzled over his unhappy marriage. He and Ann, his wife, never exchanged harsh words. He kept his

93

complaints against her to himself. He had looked at her personality and her idiosyncrasies from all angles and tried to do what would bring a balance between them. They never argued. But with all their efforts at adjustment, there was little happiness. Their approach did not work because they simply could not figure each other out. Adjustments based on this faulty approach were bound to fail. To do unto others as you would have them do to you is the opposite of trying to figure each other out.

What is it that you would like others to do unto you?
• adjust to your likes and dislikes
• express appreciation for favors done
• praise you for your achievements
• forgive you for your failures
• pay attention when you talk
• not hold you accountable for your behavior
• let you set your own rules
• provide money to spend as you wish
• tell you the truth
• maintain a neat house

Such a list requires some serious self-examination. Perhaps you should eliminate some of them or add some others. As you put your desires into practice, you will discover some of them are not really in your best interests. Your list will keep changing.

When you have completed your list, then do just that toward others. When Scott and Ann proceeded on the basis of doing to the other what each wanted done to themselves, their frustrations disappeared and they found a happy life together. Try it.

Such an attitude puts a high premium on communication. The term is used in preference to "talking," for people can do much talking and still live in a state of almost complete mental isolation. Communication means to overcome the desire to conceal feelings and thoughts and rise to the level of talking about money, fears, wishes, motivations, sexual feelings and responses, mistakes made, resentments, and misunderstandings with the intent to resolve them.

ATTITUDE

In writing to the Corinthians, Paul says,

> **For our boasting is this: the testimony of our con-
> science that we conducted ourselves in the world
> in simplicity and godly sincerity, not with fleshly
> wisdom but by the grace of God, and more
> abundantly toward you.**
> 2 CORINTHIANS 1:12

Husband and wife ought to approach each other in like manner—out of a good conscience, in simplicity and godly sincerity, by the grace of God. This is the attitude that paves the way for letting your partner know what is really on your heart.

Again, Paul says,

> **Therefore, putting away lying, [Let] each one [of
> you] speak truth with his neighbor, for we are
> members of one another.**
> EPHESIANS 4:25

Unity is based on the testimony of our conscience (2 Cor. 1:12), on being thoroughly and completely truthful with one another.

Note Ephesians 4:1–16. Here Paul speaks of the benefit given to us in order that we may become perfect in our relationships one to another.

> **. . . but, speaking the truth in love, may grow up
> in all things into Him who is the head—Christ.**
> EPHESIANS 4:15

Speaking the truth is not enough. It must be done in love, not with a vindictive spirit. Note that this verse does not address timing. Should you do it today, tomorrow, or next week?

95

Jesus once said to His disciples,

> **"I still have many things to say to you, but you
> cannot bear *them* now."**
> JOHN 16:12

He did not conceal the fact that He had more to say. But He chose
not to say it then. Perhaps they were tired. They may have been discussing something else and it was not the time to bring up a new subject.
Perhaps they were not in a receptive mood.

The golden rule makes Ephesians 5:28–29 come alive.

> **So husbands ought to love their own wives as their
> own bodies; he who loves his wife loves himself.
> For no one ever hated his own flesh, but nourishes
> and cherishes it, just as the Lord *does* the church.**
> EPHESIANS 5:28–29

There is no second guessing needed here. Such honesty involves your
behavior in God's presence. Your wife is the one who receives the benefit.

PRAISE

It is important to note that communication involves more than verbal declarations. Paul recognized the Thessalonians' work of faith, labor
of love, and patience of hope in our Lord Jesus Christ. There is the wife
who has very little to say. It is her tender glance that speaks of her love.
To cook the meals as her husband likes them is her way of expressing
her devotion. Her husband recognizes these acts as her way of communicating. To seek to understand the meaning of each other's words and
deeds and to accept them for what they mean is to be truly united.

Such communication is fundamental to a good marriage. What do
you appreciate about your partner? Be sure that you know. Then let your

partner know. What can you do for each other? Whatever it is, do it heartily, as unto the Lord.

Jerry is a fellow who makes such an effort. He married Alice fifteen years ago. Just as in courtship days, he still expresses continuously his appreciation of her cooking, the way she dresses and combs her hair, her manner with the children, her spirit of sacrifice in her church work, and her graciousness toward guests. She does not tire of hearing his praise. It is a pleasant part of life that contributes to maintaining good fellowship, just as sleep, good air, and food sustain a healthy body.

These things are done day in and day out, not as a distasteful, boring, dull, meaningless chore, but as a pleasant, helpful routine, eagerly looked forward to because they are pleasantly beneficial.

It is important to know that Jerry is expressing genuine appreciation. Knowing he is not just parroting empty, meaningless words his wife insists on hearing is significant.

On the other hand, Jerry also must continuously remind his wife that she tends to neglect housekeeping, spends too much time over coffee which throws off the timing of meals, and leans toward extravagance. He does this most of the time in patience and long-suffering. How much patience and long-suffering? Fifteen years of it so far.

Jerry is a kind man. He loves to be helpful to other people. Alice appreciates this about him and tells him so. She also keeps reminding him that she respects his faithfulness to his job and to his church and his thriftiness and careful management of family finances.

On the other hand, she must keep after him because, in his zeal to serve others, he tends to neglect the children. He is careless, too, about shining his shoes and changing his shirt often enough. Alice does this most of the time in all patience and long-suffering. How much patience and long-suffering? Fifteen years of it so far.

Why do these people not correct their ways permanently, you ask? It is a good question. I am not describing angels, but a couple who have their strengths and weaknesses and who need each other. By keeping the channels of communication open between them and with their relationship undergirded by deep love and a desire to please, each is a better person than he would be without the other. Yet there is the tendency for each to drift back into old ways.

You do not get very far seeking to conceal your negative reactions, making excuses, or seeking a scapegoat when differences arise. If the relationship is strained, you need to understand why and what can be done to improve it. When friction arises, it requires more than a description of the action that caused it. A careful sharing of how the act affected the quality of the relationship is necessary. The feelings, attitudes, and thoughts that the act aroused must be mutually understood. All this effort is useless without the intent to arrive at a mutually agreeable change.

Keeping a marriage in tune brings to mind the story a father told about his two daughters. Both were given piano lessons and both were doing very well. Then the teacher assigned them a four-hand duet. Each child learned her own part flawlessly. It was in putting the two parts together that the trouble came. Meanwhile the family endured the discords of their failure to achieve teamwork.

"Why not start over?" a troubled parent would suggest. "If you both kept the same timing, your parts ought to harmonize." And if a common feeling for the rhythm flowed between the girls, the tones they produced would be a joy to hear.

A sense of unity between two or more people is priceless, whether it produces the music of a stirring symphony or the steam-rolling tactics of a seasoned football squad.

I speak of teamwork, united action, agreement, and intimacy. The essence of democracy is the voluntary commitment of free people to a way of life arrived at by mutual consent. One writer describes freedom as the length of the leash from a chosen stake.

The apostle Paul offered a beautiful definition of teamwork in writing to the Corinthians:

> **Now I plead with you, brethren, by the name of
> our Lord Jesus Christ, that you all speak the same
> thing, and *that* there be no divisions among you,
> but *that* you be perfectly joined together in the
> same mind and in the same judgment.**
>
> 1 Corinthians 1:10

Fellowship, which amounts to comfortable relationships, springs from mutual faith, viewpoints agreed on, and approved activities.

Opposite these terms are such words as *division, contention, strife, disagreement,* and *selfishness.* Governments, churches, and families seek to eliminate such conditions from their midst. To be perfectly joined together in the same mind and in the same thought—is there a more wholesome endeavor to which to give yourself? This is the challenge for the Christian family.

But in your effort to maintain congeniality in your family, one factor in human relations must be consciously and deliberately guarded against: We tend to grow apart.

Isaiah describes man in this way:

> **We have turned, every one, to his own way.**
>
> Isaiah 53:6a

We have turned every one to his own way—this is the story of two or more people living together. It is easy for husband and wife to take up divergent paths. Nations make treaties, governments pass laws, young lovers pledge agreements, families set rules. In all these efforts we see attempts to correct the tendency to wander from a standard and go our separate ways.

The prophet Amos asks the question,

> **Can two walk together, unless they are agreed?**
>
> Amos 3:3

The psalmist reflects,

Behold, how good and how pleasant *it is*
For brethren to dwell together in unity!
PSALM 133:1

Probably no one in the field of human relations would dispute the prophet and the psalmist. The battleground comes in the process of arriving at this unity and in adhering to the standards that maintain it. There are many shades of opinion on the standards, the values, and the goals by which we should steer our lives.

Whenever two or more persons living side by side differ over a point, some kind of agreement must be reached, or there is a parting of the ways and each is the loser.

Carl walked into my office and slumped into a chair, a dejected soul. He was a success financially. But after twenty-two years of marriage, he was ready to quit, thoroughly disgusted with his wife. He had given up hunting and fishing because she did not like him doing them. They had no social life because she did not like to go out. They never fought. They just did not talk, but the silence was driving him mad. He wanted to go out but felt guilty if he did.

Rhea, his wife, shared his attitude. She was a very bitter woman and looked it.

"I can hardly stand the sight of him," she said. "We have nothing to talk about. We used to visit his friends, but he did not like the way I talked to them. He did not say much, just gave me that withering look. So I quit talking. What is the use of just sitting? I quit going out. I do not like fishing and hunting. I do not care if he goes, but he thinks I do not want him to go, I guess. He has never asked me how I feel."

These two people, intelligent, polished, and successful separately, are like the two girls playing a duet. When they sensed discord, each quit rather than mend it. Their marriage slowly ground to a halt. They were strangers to each other, isolated mentally and separated by an invisible but real barrier of resentment.

Now, however, they are on a friendly basis after having started to build a bridge of communication between them. The bridge was built by dismantling the wall made out of bitterness and selfishness. Now they can learn to walk in the Spirit. It has enabled them to define their difficulties and work them out by mutually agreeable solutions, rather than turning away from each other when signs of discord appear.

Each had been sure that to be honest with the other about feelings and opinions would blow the marriage sky-high. Instead, each found that repentance before God and drawing on His love gave them the grace necessary to begin building a mutual life.

This couple, too, illustrates the tendency of everyone to turn to his own way. People tend to grow apart more naturally than toward an open, honest sharing of viewpoints, attitudes, and feelings.

A happy marriage is not possible without communication that reveals, with reasonable certainty, how the other feels and thinks about a given action or situation. Conversing on any subject, airing any problem that might arise, and sharing with the other private fears, worries, and desires is the bedrock of marriage. And it is not always verbal. Attitudes are expressed by a smile, a frown, or a shrug of the shoulders. We sense disapproval even though the spoken words are reassuring.

Communication ceases when the need to conceal becomes stronger than the desire for unity. There is the husband who will not speak of his financial worries, so he hides his insecurity behind what he calls a "manly" silence. The wife conceals her spur-of-the-moment purchase or keeps to herself the concern that her husband no longer finds her to be attractive. Slowly, couples who once were excellent companions learn to rope off areas of their lives and live in a kind of marital no-man's-land. Conversation declines to "truce" subjects. How do you mend the broken lines of communication between husbands and wives and among members of a family?

Let us look just a little further at the elements that cause our communication to break down. There is the tendency to hide. Is it not true that we seek to protect ourselves from disapproval, that we hesitate to reveal our own selfish desires and tend to conceal our negative feelings? Yes, the tendency to conceal is summed up in three sentences by the Lord Jesus Christ.

> "And this is the condemnation, that the light has come into the world, and men loved darkness rather than light, because their deeds were evil. For everyone practicing evil hates the light and does not come to the light, lest his deeds should be exposed."
>
> JOHN 3:19–20

Again, the tendency for human relations to break down is described by Isaiah when he says "we have turned, every one, to his own way." True, we have a strong desire for fellowship, but the human heart with its deceitfulness drives us apart, making our own way a stronger attraction than a mutual way.

Suppose you do communicate your true feelings, attitudes, and desires. Communication, itself, will not necessarily produce unity. The desire for unity must be present. You may clarify your desires to your partner in order to get your own way. Your objective is to advance your own selfish ends, not to achieve unity. As a husband, you may be firmly set against your wife's idea. Communication, then, simply clarifies the issue. It does not provide a mutual solution. Undergirding this process of communication must be a firm foundation of love and unselfishness.

What of the tendency to become negative in our conversation? We can heed Jesus' advice, who a long time ago pointed out that what comes out of the mouth is a great deal more important than what goes into it.

Acknowledging Him as our Savior, the One who died for our sins, enables us to walk in the newness of life. Jesus made the statement

> "What comes out of a man, that defiles a man."
>
> MARK 7:20

He gives further explanation in verses 21 and 23:

> **"For from within, out of the heart of men, proceed evil**
> **thoughts, adulteries, fornications, murders, . . . All**
> **these evil things come from within and defile a man."**
> MARK 7:21, 23

What is it, then, that is behind negative conversations? The tendency to break fellowship by going your own way, the inclination to conceal from your most trusted companion? It is the heart of man, which the Bible describes as desperately wicked.

The answer—the Christian answer—to how you can maintain the kind of communication that leads to a mutual walk goes right back to your set of beliefs. Your set of beliefs should include
- The sinfulness of man
- Redemption from sin by faith in Christ's death
- The indwelling of the Holy Spirit, which enables us to do the will of God
- Walking in the Spirit

True Christian marriage is based on the love of God that is shed abroad in our hearts by the Holy Spirit.

> **Now hope does not disappoint, because the love**
> **of God has been poured out in our hearts by the**
> **Holy Spirit who was given to us.**
> ROMANS 5:5

That love was described in chapter 5 as working out in our actions as part of the foundation on which the Christian marriage is based. Remember these? Patience, kindness, generosity, humility, courtesy, unselfishness, good temper, guilelessness, and sincerity.

With such love as the foundation, a Christian couple can proceed to establish and maintain a mutual way of life.

Such a foundation will enable you to approach your partner with the sincere desire to know and to be known, to listen and to share, to understand and to be understood. Thus, you are ready to build the bridge across which two-way communication can flow. Two-way communication is, first of all, a matter of the Spirit. It requires two people who have been set free from the natural tendency to hide, to conceal, and to be secretive. They have been set free by acknowledging that Christ died to set them free and they are now submitting to the Holy Spirit, who keeps them as they continually yield to Him.

Communication is based on a combination of truth and love. Paul describes mature Christians for us:

> **that we should no longer be children, tossed to
> and fro and carried about with every wind of
> doctrine, by the trickery of men, in the cunning
> craftiness by which they lie in wait to deceive, but,
> speaking the truth in love, may grow up in all
> things into Him who is the head—Christ.**
> EPHESIANS 4:14–15

In this same chapter, Paul speaks of the man who is renewed in the spirit of the mind and who is created in righteousness and true holiness. To this man, Paul says,

> **Therefore, putting away lying, [Let] each one [of
> you] speak truth with his neighbor, for we are
> members of one another.**
> EPHESIANS 4:25

I have emphasized that the natural tendency is to turn everyone to his own way. You tend to become disunited and to make judgments and decisions based on what you believe to be right and what is attractive and desirable to you. The interests of the family easily become submerged in favor of your own.

Because this is true, you must depend also on the other material besides love that goes to make up the foundation undergirding a Christian marriage—the Bible. This is the standard mutually acceptable to the serious Christian couple.

**All Scripture *is* given by inspiration of God, and *is* prof-
itable for doctrine, for reproof, for correction, for
instruction in righteousness, that the man of God may
be complete, thoroughly equipped for every good work.**
2 TIMOTHY 3:16–17

The application of this standard will, however, test the very foundation of a Christian marriage. Notice the kind of communication suggested here: reproof, correction, instruction in righteousness. These are pointed words. Yet they reveal that the way to help maintain a mutual way of life is to tell your partner when he or she is wandering from your agreed-on path. This implies also your willingness to have your own wanderings brought to light.

RECONCILIATION

The time comes in a marriage when differences arise. The conversation, action, or attitude of your partner is not appreciated. Your partner will be grateful to know about this if the basic relationship between you is a healthy one. Paul wrote to the Romans,

**Now I myself am confident concerning you, my
brethren, that you also are full of goodness, filled with
all knowledge, able also to admonish one another.**
ROMANS 15:14

Partners, dedicated to building a united marriage, can each assume that the other will appreciate an admonition and will be willing to consider revising his behavior in a way that is mutually acceptable. There is a great difference between peace and the kind of cold, brittle silence that develops when partners have unspoken, unrevealed differences between them. The "silent treatment" is a far cry from unity and peace.

TAKE THE INITIATIVE IN RESTORING UNITY

It is well to review the order of your loyalties. Our first duty is to love God with all our heart, all our soul, and all our mind. If we wish to please Him, we will be careful to maintain unity with the brethren. The Lord Jesus gave us the basis for maintaining good relations.

> "Therefore if you bring your gift to the altar, and there remember that your brother has something against you, leave your gift there before the altar, and go your way. First be reconciled to your brother, and then come and offer your gift."
> MATTHEW 5:23–24

If your partner *has anything against you,* it is your move to be reconciled. It is inconceivable to think of quarreling and divisions as a part of the lives of a Christian couple. Christianity and quarreling do not go together. If you are conscious of doing something that is offensive to your partner, it is your responsibility to go to him or her and be reconciled. This is one principle of good Christian living. Otherwise, your service to God is unacceptable.

The Lord Jesus gave us another guideline for maintaining unity between two people.

> "Moreover if your brother sins against you, go and tell him his fault between you and him alone. If he hears you, you have gained your brother. But if he will not hear, take with you one or two

more, that *'by the mouth of two or three witnesses
every word may be established.'* And if he refuses
to hear them, tell *it* to the church. But if he refuses
even to hear the church, let him be to you like a
heathen and a tax collector."
MATTHEW 18:15–17

Here the shoe is on the other foot. Now your partner is at fault. It is still your move. A Christian ought to be so desirous of achieving unity that, failing to find a basis of reconciliation alone, an attempt will be made to seek help from one or two others. Failing this, the Christian ought to turn to the church. This is going a long, long way to be reconciled.

There is a caution, however, stated by Paul:

Brethren, if a man is overtaken in any trespass,
you who *are* spiritual restore such a one
in a spirit of gentleness, considering yourself
lest you also be tempted.
GALATIANS 6:1

Who is it that is to go to a person taken in fault? You who are spiritual, a person who has the fruit of the Spirit listed in Galatians 5:22–23—love, joy, peace, patience, kindness, goodness, faithfulness, gentleness, self-control—operating in your life. If you do not, you need to correct your response before you approach the other person. If you qualify, you need to rebuke the other person—that is, you need to point out the offensive or unacceptable behavior.

This principle applies to partners also. Why must this be so? You may have the best intentions in approaching your partner about some fault. However, it is possible that your partner will be sensitive about it, resent your approach, try to argue, or say things that are not complimentary. If your response is in anger, then your good intentions result in your becoming embroiled in an argument. No progress has been made toward unity if you match malice with malice, satisfying the sinful nature yourself, if you are faced by a partner who is not in the best of spirits. It is the spiritual person who can take a tongue lashing in the right way. An individual with faults of his own should look after his own faults and not after those his partner may have. You must approach your partner watching yourself, or you also may be tempted.

REBUKE AND FORGIVE

Suppose someone is repentant and still repeats undesirable behavior over and over. The Scripture says to rebuke and forgive. I found myself in this situation with my wife, Jo. Shortly after saying our marriage vows, we learned that some adjustments were necessary.

I was driving, and Jo was sitting next to me when she said, "Henry, would you please not drive so closely to the car in front of us?" I proceeded to defend my driving style and driving record. "Look, I haven't had an accident in years, and I am in better passing condition when I am close to the next car." She insisted that I was driving too close. We were clearly annoyed at each other.

Finally I saw the light. How selfish of me to ignore her request and not make driving with me more relaxing for her. I agreed to open the distance between our car and the one we were following. But I learned that driving habits are not easily changed. I would unthinkingly lapse into my old habits. Often I would remind myself; if I did not, Jo surely would. There were some trips when I needed to repent seven times in a day. After weeks of catching myself and Jo rebuking me, I developed the habit of staying the proper distance from the car in front of me. Occasionally, I need to correct and "walk in the Spirit." She needs to rebuke and forgive.

We had another adjustment to make. Jo had a habit of taking off her glasses and laying them on her lap, a table, a car seat, or any other handy place. They would slide off her lap and disappear, or she would forget where she left them. She was constantly looking for them.

This was unacceptable to me. I felt something simple could be done to solve the problem. She reluctantly agreed to put them in her purse any time she took them off while away from home. At home, there were two designated places for them. If I saw her put them down anywhere else, I would remind her on the spot. For a while it was a case of reminding her many times every day. Her response was not very friendly, and neither was my response to her response. We both had to repent of our bad attitudes. But the "rebuke-repent" process worked. It quickly became apparent that knowing where her glasses were was worth the effort on both of our parts.

These adjustments made it clear that we both needed to walk "in the Spirit" and that we need to maintain a "rebuke-repent" process to deal with occasional lapses.

RESOLVING THE PROBLEM

Julie could bring herself to tears about a disagreement with Steve and claim she was sorry about her sinful behavior toward her husband. But they both knew her tears were an expression of anger and frustration, not shame and true repentance. She was only adding deception to her list of sins.

Julie had to humble herself to the point of "loathing herself" for her unloving and judgmental attitudes. She was irritated at Steve's moodiness and outbursts of anger and condemned him for it. She finally repented, "I won't give a meaningless apology. I hate this about myself, and I don't want to be this way anymore."

I confronted Steve one night about his anger toward his wife, Julie. He did not much care for the idea that anger was a sin. "Doesn't a man have a right to be mad when he is mistreated? Any man would be angry when his wife shows him disrespect," he said. Anger was how he expressed himself. It was how he won arguments and how he kept Julie from running over him. Anger was a tool. Anger was power for him.

I asked Steve whether his tool of anger was working. "Are your arguments being resolved?" All Steve and Julie could do was look at each other with blank stares. They saw that, after five years of marriage, Steve was still angry and moody and Julie was still irritated and condemning. No, the tool of anger was not solving anything. Recurring arguments in the marriage always wound up being about the same thing.

Steve and Julie needed a better way and opted to try God's way. But could they let go of their sin? Steve knew he had been out of line after an argument. He was even sorry and asked for forgiveness. But he was never cleansed of his sin. He had never let go.

Steve could not deny the many Scriptures presented to him identifying anger as sin, especially,

> **The wrath of man does not produce the
> righteousness of God.**
> JAMES 1:20

Could it be true? Could disagreements be without anger? Could they end in a solution acceptable to both of them? In prayer, God convicted Steve of his anger. Soon he repented.

Steve found out God's forgiveness and cleansing are always available. When he feels anger and confesses it, God immediately provides forgiveness and cleansing.

Five years later Steve and Julie report that they have had no more blow-ups. What a difference God has made through their repentance! They can make the constant adjustments marriage demands because they let God replace their sinful reactions with His fruitful responses. Julie is less apt to hide her irritation with Steve, which she describes as "walking on eggshells." She is free to speak the truth in love. And when she does go her own way and condemns, God's love in Steve covers it with a simple smile. If Steve's heart is right with God, love spills out. If he has a fleshly response, Julie asks him how his spirit is. That is his cue to do a soul checkup. God's way works so much better than our own!

MARY AND NORM

Mary and Norm had just moved into a new house. The night before she had put a cake in the oven. The oven overheated and burned the cake. She called the power company to come and repair the oven. They agreed to come at 1:00 P.M. She made sure of the time. She would be away until 1:00. She needed to bake a cake for a meeting she had that night.

Mary arrived promptly at 1:00. No one showed up. Very irritated, she called the power company. They said their representative was there at 12:00 P.M. as agreed, waited a half hour, and left. By now Mary was furious and vented her wrath on the lady on the other end of the phone. She specifically agreed on 1:00.

Mary called her husband at work, expecting some sympathy. Instead, he was sympathizing with the lady from the power company. Thoroughly disgusted, she walked back and forth, fists clenched, breathing heavily, and grinding her teeth.

Then she saw the light. Her hostile response was a signal to pay more attention to her relationship with God. She was not walking in the Spirit. A repentant prayer cleansed her heart and filled it with God's joy and love. She made a quick phone call to the lady at the power company to apologize for the way she talked to her. The lady thought Mary was not a normal customer. She had never received an apology. Mary made her day.

Then Mary called her husband. She thanked him for rebuking her, as it made her aware of how angry she was. Now she was basking in the freedom from a troubled heart.

You will save yourself many tensions, troubles, and difficulties if you follow through on the biblical rules for getting along together. Your approach should be with the assumption that your partner is "full of goodness" and happy for any admonition that will aid in a clearer understanding between you. Your approach should be with the purpose that

**if it is possible, as much as depends on you, live
peaceably with all men.**
ROMANS 12:18

Your approach should be with the intent of being reconciled and not to vent repressed, negative, sinful emotions. If your partner's response is in (sinful) anger, it is your good spirit that is important.

When differences come, there is the tendency to leave your first love for God, to forsake prayer, and to turn to the sinful nature for a solution. To win your point becomes the important goal. The effort at reconciliation, carried out in the sinful nature, will result in failure to adjust to change. Partners may turn away from making an adjustment. Or they may try and fail.

INCIPIENT STAGE

When couples realize that an adjustment cannot be made, this is a red light. If neglected, this will destroy the marriage. This is called the incipient stage. It is at this point that the partners ought to turn to someone qualified to give counsel. Otherwise, they will attempt to evade or forget the area of conflict. They may try to insulate it by ignoring it. They may treat the conflict as a sensitive spot that they try not to touch. Conflicts or differences may not arise over such matters as extreme cruelty or immorality. They can be differences over such things as neatness, cleanliness, clothing, and friends. One young couple agreed to buy the most expensive BMW, but disagreed violently over keeping candy or peanuts in a dish in the living room. This is not a happy marriage. Both husband and wife feel hostility (sinfulness) that cannot be released; they feel upset or disappointed.

CHRONIC STAGE

Soon one of them begins to lose heart and hope. Marriage is not meeting his or her basic needs. A partner will soon begin to wonder how else these needs can be met and will look for outlets outside the marriage. This is called the chronic stage.

BE KIND AND COMPASSIONATE TO ONE ANOTHER

Your marriage will become a happy, mutually satisfactory one if both of you set your sights on unity, ministering to each other and communicating with each other in the proper spirit. As Christians, you will find strength to do this as you pray and as you remember the exhortation:

> **And be kind to one another, tenderhearted, forgiving one another, just as God in Christ also forgave you.**
> EPHESIANS 4:32

INFORMATION AND INSPIRATION

Partners can be drawn closer together through sharing with each other their experiences, thoughts, desires, longings, plans, and weaknesses.

Husbands and wives need to inform, challenge, and inspire one another. Here are some suggestions:

> **But exhort one another daily, while it is called *"Today,"* lest any of you be hardened through the deceitfulness of sin.**
> HEBREWS 3:13

> **Finally, brethren, whatever things are true, whatever things are noble, whatever things *are* just, whatever things *are* pure, whatever things *are* lovely, whatever things *are* of good report, if *there is* any virtue and if *there is* anything praiseworthy—meditate on these things.**
> PHILIPPIANS 4:8

A wealthy automobile dealer tells his unhappy story. Twenty-five years ago, he and his wife were delighted when they received a profitable dealership. He worked hard day and night to build up the business. His wife was busy with the three children. The dealership prospered. As it grew in size, he became busier and busier. Soon he became interested in civic affairs and for business reasons joined various clubs. As he prospered, his wife was able to have help in the house. She joined her own clubs and various women's activities. Husband and wife, in their prosperity, developed their own separate worlds. He had very little to do with rearing the family, apart from providing a very comfortable home and plenty of money. Today, twenty-five years later, this gentleman is growing old, his children are gone, and he and his wife have nothing in common. He is a very lonely man, even though he lives in luxurious surroundings.

This need not happen to any marriage. Be sure to take the time to have fellowship together as partners and as a family. You can maintain common interests. You can share reading materials. You can share church activities. You can share the task of parenthood. This is a mutual task, not the wife's exclusive area. As partners who have a mind to keep in step, you will find ways to accomplish this. Remember that the tendency to build separate worlds is a natural one. To prevent this from happening, you must deliberately and consciously have a plan and make it work.

Our emphasis has been on helps for partners who are purposed in their hearts to establish a sound marriage. These principles will produce few results for those who use them in an attempt to get their own way. They will be truly effective for those who seek a mutual, united, like-minded partnership.

The objective is a meeting of minds. If your minds are not together, you are not together. Being touched by someone you are at odds with can be unbearable. A client told me she could hardly stand driving her top-of-the-line Mercedes because it was a present from her husband whom she despised. Not to be like-minded is a violation of God's law—a sin.

A simple, repentant prayer for forgiveness and cleansing of selfishness and lack of love is the key to swiftly eliminating disagreements.

CHAPTER 6

Walking Together in Unity

... being knit together in love ...
COLOSSIANS 2:2A

Behold, how good and how pleasant *it is*
For brethren to dwell together in unity!
PSALM 133:1

... submitting to one another in the fear of God.
EPHESIANS 5:21

Can two walk together, unless they are agreed?
AMOS 3:3

In our day the relationship of men to women is a very "touchy" subject. *Together* and *submission* and "till death do us part" are delicate words.

A new day has dawned for women. *Independence* and *equality* are words that apply to marriage, some maintain. Any book on a biblical approach to marriage must sooner or later face this verse:

. . . submitting to one another in the fear of God.
EPHESIANS 5:21

AGREE TO DISAGREE

One idea of unity and agreement is expressed in the words: *agree to disagree.* This idea is based on placing a high value on individuality. In a democracy you must respect the rights of the individual. This is understood by some to mean that you must accept each other just as they are. According to this philosophy, if the wife thinks differently from her husband in some areas, she has every right to go on doing so. The husband has a right to hold different views from his wife. Each must be gracious and understanding toward the other, but each should grant the other the right to be different.

A hundred years ago, domestic life was virtually the only option of a woman. Today, a woman can be as self-sufficient as any man. She has a wide variety of careers to choose from. Jobs are available for married as well as for single women. In addition, a vast world of clubs, social service, and church work beckons.

The challenge of a varied life, continuous emphasis on the equality of the sexes, easy mobility, the telephone, fax, and e-mail all contribute to make the role of "wife" as difficult for the woman to keep in balance as the role of "husband" is for the man.

Strangely, in our day a host of people think of freedom in marriage as complete individuality without leadership. All couples, soon after marriage, find that a relationship of "power struggles" is most difficult, if not impossible.

At her insistence, Jim and Beth pledged mutual respect for each other's rights when they were married. In their early years, if he differed with her choice of friends, social life, style of clothing, or religious life, she invoked the "freedom" amendment. "We must be broad-minded, not imposing one's personal beliefs and standards on another," she would remind him.

Over the years Jim gradually conceded to her. Both became unbending and self-centered. She made her own life in parties, travel, and fashions. He made his in business, civic endeavors, and hobbies. They were clearly traveling separate paths.

The novelty of new things wears off, and Beth began to feel the need for a companionship that neither money nor friends could give. She needed to "belong," to share. So she turned back to her husband, suggesting they do things together, asking his opinions about her decisions and plans.

Now Jim invoked the "freedom" amendment. He had set his course and did not care to change it. She was free to do what she wanted. There was no praise or blame from him. She has the absolute freedom of a lonely life. Now she did not want it. The foundation of this marriage was all wrong. When one partner takes a divergent path from the other, the distance between those paths will widen.

Jim and Sharon discovered the emptiness of self-seeking. Jim was consistently punctual. When he said eight o'clock, he meant eight-zero-zero. Sharon was always late. So Jim sat there and fumed disgustedly.

Down the steps came Sharon. She looked lovely. Her figure, beautiful eyes, sparkling smile . . . all something to behold. She bounded across the room, her inviting arms outstretched. Suddenly, Jim forgot his griping. His whole body experienced a pleasant sensation as she touched his hand. Then Sharon would cuddle up to Jim, and all he could see ahead of him was a wonderful evening with a delightful girl.

Occasionally, while they were sitting alone talking, he asked her, "Honey, are you going to be late like this after we are married?" Sharon would cuddle up to Jim, look up at him seductively, and say, "Would it really matter to you if I were late after we get married? Would you love me anyway?"

"Honey," he would say in a burst of daring confidence, "I would love you no matter what you did!"

So the punctual young man married the wistful maiden of his dreams, promising to love her no matter what! When Jim woke up the first morning after the honeymoon, he bounded out of bed at the first ring of the alarm and, minutes later, emerged from the bathroom washed, shaved, dressed, and ready for breakfast. But where was his wife? He did a double take. She was still in bed!

"Come on! Come on!" he called to his sweetheart. "Aren't you going to have any breakfast?" From beneath the cover came a sleepy sigh. "You can get something at the donut shop on your way to work. I don't have to get up yet."

She had her own schedule and was not in that much of a hurry. But he pressured her more every day. When they were getting ready to go anywhere, he pushed her and offered time checks until her nerves nearly snapped. This same couple had said only a few months earlier, "We are the perfect couple. One is punctual; the other is late. We will balance each other. We will even improve each other."

It sounded reasonable. But now Jim had interpreted her pokiness as a subtle feminine whack at his masculine authority. She saw his pushiness as unnecessary nagging.

There were other disagreements, and all followed a pattern. Jim would fume a few days, then bring up the subject. Sharon would cuddle up to him, ask him to declare his love for her, then keep on doing her own thing. Jim would contain himself a few days, then force another discussion and angrily spill out his opinion. Sharon would counter. After a few exchanges, the conversation would grind to a disgusted silence with no solution.

Every attempt ended in a hopeless deadlock. Sharon and Jim made the same mistake thousands of other married couples have made. They arrived at the tragic conclusion: they were mismatched.

"He does not understand me," Sharon sobbed.

"She does not care about me," came Jim's snarling reply.

Only a few months earlier, he had tingled all over just thinking about Sharon. And she had happily melted into those big, strong arms and stood on tiptoe to kiss him lingeringly. Now they could not stand to touch each other.

Declaring their love and wanting to get along had not created harmonious relations. Nor had the ecstasy of sexual relations. Instead, self-seeking and acts of the sinful nature (resentment and anger) had cooled the thrill of physical contact and thrown up a wall between them.

UNITY BETWEEN PARTNERS IS PLANNED— AGREE TO AGREE

A smoothly working marriage requires teamwork. It is necessary that both the husband and the wife agree on what the place of the husband should be. It is necessary that both husband and wife agree on what the place of the wife should be. Marriage is more than a working agreement between two equal parties. It is rather a complementary union of two members, male and female, each of whom has a special responsibility. There should not be competition between husband and wife. Each has a definite, distinct place. The roles of husband and wife fit together like two interlocking pieces of a jigsaw puzzle.

The ideal relationship between people is expressed by Paul:

> . . . **submitting to one another in the fear of God.**
> EPHESIANS 5:21

THE RULES ARE SET

A leader is necessary whenever two or more people must or intend to cooperate. Take tennis, for example. Guidelines are the tennis court and the rules. These already exist.

In singles, you have your own side of the court all to yourself. You do anything you please within the rules, without consulting or considering anyone else. You can charge the net or play back, to the right or left. You do your own thing. The idea is to outplay, outsmart, or outmaneuver each other. You win or lose, and it is fun to compete.

Suppose you and your best friend team up to play doubles. When you hop over the net, it is the same court, same equipment, and the same players. The same rules apply. Now you must cooperate instead of competing. You are teammates instead of opponents, and you can only partially do your own thing. You would collide if you both went after the ball. If you were both in the same place, your opponents would place the ball out of your reach. In order to play smoothly together, you work out a strategy: who plays right, who plays left. Most of these decisions are obvious.

If you play doubles in tennis, it is fun if decisions are agreeable and can be made quickly and easily. You determine how you cooperate on the court and within the rules.

You need a captain to call the shots when there is a question. Choosing the captain is up to the two of you. If you cannot work out a choice, you will not enjoy playing doubles.

"BEFORE MARRIAGE, WE COULD DISCUSS ANYTHING!"

Courtship is like playing singles. You are good friends. You discuss, even debate, many subjects—money, cars, politics, goals, values, neatness, dress, religion, or just about anything. You especially enjoy it when you end up on opposite sides of a subject without disturbing each other's goodwill. Both freely express opinions, but you do not have to reach an agreement.

Points of difference that are frequently mentioned by marriage partners are housekeeping, punctuality, the flavoring of the food, how often the grass should be cut, bedtime, discipline of the children, paint versus wallpaper, color schemes, entertainment, and so on.

Minor differences often cause the relationship between husband and wife to be strained. Efforts at resolving them can fail if one partner wants to go his or her own way. To agree to disagree is a wishful thought that cannot be successfully and happily carried out if there is no cooperation.

AGREE TO AGREE

> . . . fulfill my joy by being like-minded, having the
> same love, *being* of one accord, of one mind.
> PHILIPPIANS 2:2

In other words, both partners will agree to agree. It is not enough to understand and appreciate the points of difference. The goal should be to resolve those differences, to find a basis for mutual agreement.

IN MARRIAGE THE RULES ARE CREATED

You come into marriage from two different backgrounds. The husband's family had a different set of rules than his wife's. Now the two of you must do something you have probably never done before: create your own boundaries, rules, and leadership style. You probably do not have any previous experience to prepare you for this. You may have no idea how to set up boundaries and rules, much less live by them.

We go to college or trade school to prepare for our jobs, but there is no formal degree certifying us for marriage. You probably thought two married people in love automatically get along.

Then you get married. The same subjects come up for discussion: money, cars, goals, values, neatness, dress, and religion. But now it is different. I have heard many couples say, "We could discuss anything before we were married. Now we quarrel half the time."

Exactly.

Before you were married, all you had to do was have a discussion. Now you must make a decision. Before, you could end the discussion and go your own way—just like playing your half of the court in singles.

When you marry, you not only discuss questions or issues, you must come to agreements and cooperate. You can only partially do your own thing. This does not mean a loss of individuality. It does mean a voluntary commitment on the part of husband and wife to draw on personal individuality to develop a mutual way of life. The first step toward unity is that of accepting the lifetime goal of becoming like-minded, having the same love, and being one in spirit and purpose.

The relationship between a man and his wife is to be submissive and in subjection. Somehow many men and women in our day consider these words to mean disrespect and disregard for the interests and abilities of the woman. Thus, in deference to the democratic spirit, the word *obey* is eliminated from many marriage ceremonies with the magnanimous consent of the bridegroom, because to obey is an unreasonable expectation of a wife.

The terms *submission, subjection,* and *obedience* take on a more positive meaning when applied to a business. Perhaps when regarded in this light, *obey* still belongs in the marriage vow and Paul's instruction is not out of date.

The relationship of husband to wife can be likened to the relationship between two banker friends. One is president of the bank; the other is first vice president. They have worked together in this bank for thirty years. Only one of them can be president. Both, however, carry heavy responsibilities. The first vice president knows the policies as well as the president knows them. The vice president helped make them, is in accord with them, and is limited in his decisions by them. He can step in and take over at any time, and the bank will go on as before.

The longer these men work together, the clearer and more firmly established become the policies. Freedom comes through *submission, subjection,* and *obedience* to the policies. Because the policies are clear, there is never any doubt who is president, but the president depends heavily on the first vice president to help carry them out. It is a friendly relationship.

Occasionally, circumstances arise that have never come up before. The president calls his first vice president and other high officers together to ponder the question. It is a serious moment when a meeting of minds may be impossible. Such an occurrence is rare, but when a time of indecision with the vice president comes, the president must make the decision, not according to a personal whim, but in the best interests of the bank. Once the decision is made, everyone, including the president, is bound by it. If, later, the decision proves not to be in the best interests of the bank, he will change it.

It would be foolish for these two friends to haggle over who makes the decision every time the occasion demands a decision. If there were feuds, arguments, power struggles, pouting spells, or double standards, it would be a poorly run bank. Not so with these two men. There is loyalty, goodwill, confidence, and deep understanding between them.

Neither of these men is limited to this one bank to exercise his professional skills. There are other jobs in other banks that are equally challenging. But they have chosen this bank. They concentrate on the job at hand. They are faithful. They willingly submit to the bank's policies. Their decisions are in terms of the objectives and best interests of the bank, not their own interests.

Should not the role of wife be similar to that of the first vice president? The husband is the head of the wife, but this should be on the basis of friendship, loyalty, and goodwill. Family policies should be ones she has helped make, is in accord with, and is limited by. I believe it to be a reasonable thing for the wife to be consulted and her opinions seriously considered when there is a decision to be made. Selfish interest has no place in the marriage. Both husband and wife must subject themselves to the best interests and objectives of the marriage.

Many women are brilliant, talented, able administrators blessed with good judgment. They should expect their talents to be used in the best interests of the marriage.

Freedom comes through *submission, subjection,* and *obedience* to a way of life that both helped to make. That is, you both willingly choose to be yoked together in Christ as oxen plowing your field in life:

> **"Take My yoke upon you and learn from Me, for
> I am gentle and lowly in heart, and you will find
> rest for your souls."**
> MATTHEW 11:29

ELAINE'S STORY

Kerry and I have had many crises to face in our twenty-four years of marriage. However, in the midst of many trials and hardships, we have experienced the peace and joy of God. We have been through many difficult times together. Upon having Jason, our son, we discovered that we could not have any more children. For some this may sound like a blessing. For me, it was a great disappointment, for my desire was to have at least five.

Moving away to attend college was full of surprises. Everything we owned was packed in the smallest trailer you could rent and the back of a pick-up truck. Before we reached the halfway point of our trip, the truck broke down. All of this was taking place in the rain. When we finally arrived, the offices were closed and we could not get into our place. After several hours which seemed like days, we finally found a person with the key to our new home. What a sight! Kerry, Jason (age one), and I would be living in temporary housing left from World War II. Our new address was "Hut 6." This little hut, with its water-marked walls, allowed us to experience nature from inside. In the winter, snow blew through the gaps between the walls and the roof, and in the spring grass and weeds grew up behind the trim on the floor. Our hut was quite ugly, yet we thought it was cute and it became home to us. How could that be? How can one stay filled with peace and joy in the midst of something like this?

Two of the times we moved to serve on staff at churches, we discovered upon arrival that the apartment we were to call our home was not yet available. After two months of living with someone else, we moved to a nice apartment. At one apartment, we discovered that we were not the only ones living there. Our apartment was roach infested, which meant emptying cabinets and closets, covering everything, and fumigating. After going through this routine three times, all was under control. I'll never forget the time when all of our things stayed packed in a trailer covered with plastic and sat in the pastor's back yard for a month while we waited on an apartment to become available.

Another memorable moment was when our home was invaded. Home alone and recovering from surgery, I was attacked by a man whose motives were rape and possibly murder. God delivered me on both counts. How do you stay filled with peace and joy when someone is trying to kill you? Shortly after this happened, we moved to a new location and purchased our first home. Seven years later, we had to sell our house. Selling a house would not have been so bad except we ended up losing all of our equity and borrowing seven thousand dollars to go to closing.

These are just a few of the storms that we have walked through together with a unity of heart and mind. Philippians 2:2–4 is a passage of Scripture which describes what we experienced:

> **Fulfill my joy by being like-minded, having the same love, being of one accord, of one mind. *Let* nothing *be done* through selfish ambition or conceit, but in lowliness of mind let each esteem others better than himself. Let each of you look out not only for his own interests, but also for the interests of others.**

Recently however, I encountered one of the greatest struggles of my life. We had both worked on church staff for many years. Almost overnight we had a change of assignment. Kerry was traveling and speaking, and I was working on staff at our church directing preschool and children's ministries. I was seeing God at work in the lives of children, so surely this was what I should be doing. As Kerry received more and more speaking invitations, there was more need and opportunity for me to travel with him. To a busy work schedule, I added travel. Many trips to the airport and much travel began to make it impossible for me to keep up my work at the church. Work at the church was making it impossible for me to keep up with my husband and my home.

Not knowing what the problem was, I found that I would return from each trip with a terrible attitude, which always surfaced at work. At the time I did not realize that I was returning with a bad attitude because I was resenting having to leave. Finally I discovered that there was no way for me to remain working and travel with my husband, too.

Physically, this schedule would kill me. Surely this was not the kind of life Jesus spoke of.

"Take My yoke upon you and learn from Me, for I am gentle and lowly in heart, and you will find rest for your souls."
MATTHEW 11:29

So I did what I thought a "good wife" would do, and I quit my job to take care of my husband. What I discovered about myself was that outwardly I had done what I needed to do, but on the inside I was angry and resentful that I would have to give up what I had loved and had done for so many years to live out of a suitcase and sit for hours in uncomfortable chairs in conferences. I felt I was being wasted. I will never forget trying to study in preparation for leading a conference on "I Want to Enjoy My Children." The first part of that book speaks much about the husband and wife relationship. As I read, I became more and more irritated. When I came to the part about the husband and the wife reaching a point of standoff in a decision, the following Scripture was printed:

Wives, submit to your own husbands, as to the Lord.
EPHESIANS 5:22

I slammed the book shut and threw it on the floor saying, "God, You are not fair; You always side with men!"

Though I did not realize it, many of my friends were praying for me during this difficult time. My husband remained faithful to God and continued to love me and pray for me. My pastor had made himself available to help me. At first I was angry at him for insinuating that I was angry.

Sitting at the table with Dr. Brandt, I said, "I am seeing that I am kind of independent. I did not know I was like this." His comment to me was, "Independence will only breed more independence, and one day you will wake up and find yourself a very lonely, independent person." This one statement caused me to think a great deal. I could see that Kerry was going in one direction and I was going in another.

Can two walk together, unless they are agreed?
AMOS 3:3

Other things happened that same week that caused anger to surface in me, and through this I saw that what my pastor had said about me was true. I called and asked for his help. He shared much with me about the role of the wife, and I decided that men must be the most selfish creatures on the face of the earth!

Then, he challenged me with this question: "Elaine, what could God do through Kerry's life if you would pour all of this time and energy into being a godly woman and the wife to Kerry that God wants you to be?" As though fearful of being hit, he very quickly inserted, "Now, I'm not saying you are not a godly woman." As I began tossing that question over in my mind, I began to see that I was the selfish one. I had not been at all concerned about what God could do through the life of my husband but only about what I wanted to do. My heart broke over what I saw in me. In order to be that kind of wife to Kerry, I had to get rid of all my selfishness, and I knew that only God could do this.

I asked God to forgive me and cleanse me of selfishness, anger, and resentment and to fill my heart with love, joy, peace, kindness, and goodness. The peace and unity that we had experienced for years was suddenly restored.

Behold, how good and how pleasant *it is*
For brethren to dwell together in unity!
PSALM 133:1

God has given me a whole new desire and has shown me that Kerry is my ministry.

"So then, they are no longer two but one flesh.
Therefore what God has joined together, let not
man separate."
MATTHEW 19:6

Their story beautifully illustrates the truth:

Behold, how good and how pleasant *it is*
For brethren to dwell together in unity!
PSALM 133:1

The husband and wife should set policies and practices that bind them both. As the marriage goes on, duties and responsibilities of each should become increasingly clear and more firmly established.

Occasionally, circumstances will arise when a meeting of minds will not be possible. A couple walking along a mutually agreed-on pathway will come to a fork. The husband will want to go one way, his wife the other, each believing the goal lies at the end of the route he or she would choose. One must make the decision and the other yield, or the two will find themselves walking separate paths and the distance between those paths will widen as they continue on. Even compromise has its final point of concession. At such a time, the husband will carefully make the decision. This is assuming, of course, loyalty and respect and dedication between a couple.

Freedom comes through *submission, subjection,* and *obedience* to a way of life that both helped to make. If you accept the Bible as your guidebook, then you as the husband will take the lead and you as the wife will give it to him.

Dozens of women have come to my consulting office because of a strained marriage. A chief reason for the strain was that a difference of opinion arose in the marriage and neither partner would concede. Case after case shows that many women are not content, even if their husbands give up the direction of the home to them. Neither are they content to rebel. With such reaction becoming an established pattern in wife-run homes, it appears that even with its voice of divine authority laid aside for the moment, the Bible has the common-sense slant on how a man and woman can best live together.

Consider the beauty of Paul's challenge:

> Now I plead with you, brethren, by the name of
> our Lord Jesus Christ, that you all speak the same
> thing, and *that* there be no divisions among you,
> but *that* you be perfectly joined together in the
> same mind and in the same judgment.
>
> 1 CORINTHIANS 1:10

In our day, the wife faces a major change as she begins in marriage. She must often interrupt a career, a busy, fascinating, varied life involving contact with many interesting people. She may assume the role of homemaker, as well as working outside the home, which is a startling change of pace.

Many wives indulge in self-pity, longing for their former ways of life rather than proceeding to make the adjustments that are necessary. But on the other hand, there are hundreds of thousands of happy wives. And not one of them has a perfect husband! Experience shows that marriage is a step up, not a step down. Why? Because the busy life of the single woman can lose its fascination, although women not in this situation may find it hard to believe.

Submission to the task of being a wife is not the end of freedom, but the beginning of one of the highest and most challenging of professions. There is routine work as wife and mother just as in any profession. Think of the number of throats, ears, and nostrils that a doctor looks into every day. We do not feel sorry for the doctor because he does not feel sorry for himself. He is a member of perhaps the most respected of professions. Yet he has endless routine work to do.

The wife, like the doctor, will become a contented person as she sees beyond the routine to the satisfaction gained from effective service to others, in her case, to husband and children. Self-interest is incompatible with effective service, marriage, or parenthood.

One of the major tasks of a woman, then, is to study the role of a wife and keep it in balance amid many counter attractions.

THE CERTAINTY OF UNCERTAINTY

One of the dependable features of marriage is the certainty of uncertainty. One of the great tasks facing marriage partners is that of accepting the fact of change. In a marriage, there is a continual series of changing events which demand a constant adjustment of both husband and wife. Pregnancy, the arrival of each child, the absence of children, moving, neighborhood changes, church responsibilities to assume or to give up, the shifting scene at school—these are some of the changes that come to each couple, with their corresponding adjustments.

At times husbands or wives say their partner does not seem like the person they married. Of course not. Just as your children keep changing as they grow up, so do you. At the age of one, your children act one way; at two, another way; at three, still another way; at five, differently again. A married person certainly cannot complain about lack of variety. There is a continuous change.

We must remember, however, that a marriage sometimes will develop in one way when we want it to go in another way. At such times there may be periods of disorganization when one solution is attempted, and then another, over a period of weeks or months. The chapters in a marriage are often unexpected and unpredictable. To expect an unchanging partner or unchanging circumstances, to expect to live happily ever after automatically as in the fairy tales, is not true for this life. To expect a permanent point of perfect adjustment and happiness is unrealistic. There is no family on earth that has had this experience. Continuous change is the normal experience in any marriage. This means that there must be continuous adjustment. This can be done with tenderness and compassion if you realize that the family is not a static organization. Marriage takes work. It does not just tick along in perpetual, unhindered motion. Satisfactory adjustment requires proper and free communication. It means sharing joys, giving praise, and taking admonition or correction. It means we must strive for complete understanding among all the members of the family. This is not an easy task. However, it is a workable way and leads to a peaceful, joyful life together. When the unexpected happens to you, just remember that this is no exception. This is normal. Your peace and happiness depend on your relationship to God. His peace is available during uncertain, unexpected times as well as during certain, stable times. You are not alone. The Father is with you.

Unity and agreement must be maintained. Paul says to us:

> **I, therefore, the prisoner of the Lord, beseech you
> to have a walk worthy of the calling with which
> you were called, with all lowliness and gentleness,
> with longsuffering, bearing with one another in
> love, endeavoring to keep the unity of the Spirit in
> the bond of peace.**
> EPHESIANS 4:1–3

Dedication to this goal is only the beginning. A husband and a wife have a lifelong task ahead of them. Any organization needs constant attention to keep it running smoothly. Any team must practice constantly in order to win the game. A marriage, too, needs constant attention in order to preserve unity and agreement, because changes occur inevitably in any marriage.

VERBAL AND MENTAL UNITY

Words are the means of revealing your innermost self to your partner.

> **Pleasant words *are like* a honeycomb,
> Sweetness to the soul and health to the bones.**
> PROVERBS 16:24

Differences that arise between two partners need not constitute a major crisis. Pleasant words, exchanged in the proper spirit between two people rightly related to each other, can easily bring a meeting of minds. Words can be misunderstood, however. Partners must be sure that misunderstandings do not develop or continue because of differences in the definition of words. Words like *thrift, neat, polite,* and *considerate* can have a wide range of meanings. Each partner needs to be quick to acknowledge if misunderstandings of words become evident. Your constant, continuing purpose should be to understand and to clarify rather than to justify or defend yourself.

Recently, I learned a lesson about sincere behavior with the wrong understanding of a problem. My wife and I were checking in our bags at the airport. My wife excitedly said a bag was missing. I pointed to a black bag. She said that one was not the one. That bag looked exactly like ours. She meant that the missing bag was not the black one.

We had an hour before flight time, so I got a cab and raced home to get the black bag. It was not there. So I raced back to the airport to catch my flight.

When we arrived at our destination, we went to baggage claim. Moving down the belt at baggage claim came our black bag. My wife said again that it was not the black bag that was missing. She had another one in mind. I had seen the one she wanted when I raced home, but I had a black bag in mind.

I had spent over fifty dollars cab fare racing home with a black bag in mind. My good intentions did not make up for misunderstanding what bag my wife meant.

Your goal should be that expressed by Paul in his prayer:

> **Now may the God of patience and comfort grant
> you to be like-minded toward one another, according
> to Christ Jesus, that you may with one mind
> *and* one mouth glorify the God and Father of our
> Lord Jesus Christ.**
> ROMANS 15:5–6

We are to think alike—to glorify God with one mind and one mouth. This is one of the basic tasks of marriage partners. Of course it did not seem so then, but when my wife and I think about how harried we were and how we wasted all that money for the wrong black bag, it does seem comical. It is fun to flirt and tease with each other about silly issues, but sarcasm crosses the line. How often do we get annoyed at our spouses and ridicule them in public about a past mistake, a shortcoming, or a bad habit? Comments like "She'd be late for her own funeral," or "He's like a bull in a china closet," can really dig at the heart. Disagreements must be dealt with on a timely basis with humility and good-natured tolerance, so we get on with glorifying God together.

UNITY IN FEELINGS AND EMOTIONS

This is the area of attraction or repulsion. There are many unhappy marriages among partners who have the ability to express themselves clearly and have brilliant minds, but who are unable to find within themselves a congenial spirit toward each other. A clear understanding of the thinking behind the behavior of your partner will not necessarily produce wholesome feelings and emotions. Why? Because

> . . . the fruit of the Spirit is love, joy, peace, long-
> suffering, kindness, goodness, faithfulness, gentle-
> ness, self-control. Against such there is no law.
> GALATIANS 5:22–23

Partners will find emotional unity only as they submit to a power outside of themselves—the power of God through Christ. Then they can attain to the standard set by Paul:

> *Be* kindly affectionate to one another with brotherly
> love, in honor giving preference to one another.
> ROMANS 12:10

Such a relationship cannot be developed by understanding or training or insight. Being cordial, helpful, and tolerant is not the same as yielding your life to God. It is more a matter of the will than the intellect.

To illustrate, a wife explained that she was unable to find a congenial relationship with her husband. They were both well educated and cultured. They understood each other perfectly. There were no arguments. He was a good provider. He took her wherever she wanted to go. He helped around the house. But he kept himself aloof, maintaining a cold silence most of the time. When they did speak, he was cordial and polite but said as little as possible.

The husband explained that his wife insisted on having her own way. Whenever he differed with her, there was an argument. His only solution was to keep quiet. He did what needed to be done to satisfy her demands. She could never see his side of anything, nor did she consider his needs. He despised her, but for the children's sakes he held his peace. "When the children marry," he said, "I plan to leave her." Meanwhile, he was making every effort to keep peace in the family. His idea of peace was silence. He and his wife were miles apart in their inward reactions. As the psalmist said,

> *The words* of his mouth were smoother than butter,
> But war *was* in his heart;
> His words were softer than oil,
> Yet they *were* drawn swords.
> PSALM 55:21

The solution to such a relationship lies in the acceptance by each partner of the fact that both lack the congenial spirit that will enable them to live together in peace. To achieve such unity is to turn to the source—God—who enables us to bear the fruit of the Spirit.

EFFECT OF UNITY ON THE FAMILY

When there are children in the family, unity is the foundation stone for happy family living. When there is disagreement between partners, what happens to the child? Which way will the child go? When there is a difference in outlook between a mother and a father, the child is caught in the middle. He cannot win. He can please mother or father, but he cannot please both. Here is the crux of much of the strain and tension in modern adolescents who do not know which way to turn. They must learn to play a game that appeases both mother and father. This is one of the reasons Paul said,

> **Be of the same mind toward one another. Do not
> set your mind on high things, but associate with
> the humble. Do not be wise in your own opinion.**
> ROMANS 12:16

This can be done, but it will be done only in the lives of those people who are willing to submit one to the other and to the Lord.

CHAPTER 7

Commitment and Cooperation

. . . submitting to one another in the fear of God.
EPHESIANS 5:21

**Let each of you look out not only for his own
interests, but also for the interests of others.**
PHILIPPIANS 2:4

One of the joys of my life is helping couples turn the word *submission* from a rather degrading word into a warm, friendly, satisfying word. Submission is the will to cooperate—loyalty, good-natured tolerance.

It is pleasant to listen to a couple describe their marriage when cooperation, like-mindedness, and agreement exist. Their eyes shine, their voices ring with satisfaction, even their skin glows.

On the other hand, when couples describe disagreement, discord, or conflict, I watch faces turn white, red, blue, purple. I listen to angry, vicious, verbal tirades or observe hostile silence. Their backs stiffen, jaws become set, and eyes become slits.

PARTNERS

Let us compare a marriage partnership with playing doubles in tennis. Part of the fun of playing doubles is good will and friendship, a willingness to play according to the rules, and the will to develop teamwork between the partners.

In doubles, you blend your skills. One partner may have a good forehand, the other a good backhand. This determines your playing position on the court, but then it takes weeks and months of practice to develop a cooperative style.

You work independently as well as cooperatively. When the ball is in your area, you are on your own. You make good and poor shots, causing your partner to admire—or tolerate—your efforts. You make quick decisions according to your agreed-upon plan. At times it may be necessary to alter your plan.

Now let us switch from cooperation in tennis to cooperation in marriage.

Cooperation means pleasure if you meet the conditions:
• Good will and friendship
• Pleasant anticipation
• The will to play by the rules
• The will to choose a captain
• The will to develop teamwork

To put it in a Bible verse:

. . . submitting to one another in the fear of God.
EPHESIANS 5:21

A FIRM FOUNDATION

What do you have to start with? The advantage is yours if you are a child of God. Let us review what has happened to you. The Bible says,

**Therefore, having been justified by faith, we have
peace with God through our Lord Jesus Christ.**
ROMANS 5:1

Justified? What does justified mean? Here is what you, a justified person, have done:

1. You have rcognized the fact that your sins (self-seeking and deeds of the flesh) have separated you from God (Isa. 59:2).
2. You have believed by faith that God has placed your sins on Jesus (2 Cor. 5:21; Gal. 3:13).
3. By inviting Jesus to come into your life, you have been forgiven. You are a child of God and can walk into His presence as though you never sinned, talk to Him, and expect Him to help you (John 1:12).

A NEW RESOURCE

How can God's resources help you? Here is the good news:

**Now hope does not disappoint, because the love
of God has been poured out in our hearts by the
Holy Spirit who was given to us.**
ROMANS 5:5

The love which produces harmonious living is not generated between people. It comes from outside yourself and starts with God's love. Whether you received Christ long ago or just today, you have access to His love. Ask Him to bathe your heart with it. You will be amazed at the change in your reactions to the people around you.

REMEMBER THOSE VOWS?

Remember your wedding ceremony? The vows went something like this: "Dearly beloved, we are gathered together in the sight of God . . ."

Marriage is God's idea. Remember His words?

> **And the LORD God said, "*It is* not good that man**
> **should be alone; I will make him a helper**
> **comparable to him."**
> GENESIS 2:18

Then you declared your intentions toward each other: "Will you love her, comfort her, honor and keep her . . . in sickness and in health; and forsaking all others, keep thee only unto her so long as you both shall live? I . . . take you . . . to have and to hold from this day forward, for better, for worse, for richer, for poorer, in sickness and in health, to love and to cherish, till death us do part . . ."

That ceremony suggests that

1. You are ready to start with each other as you are, not pending reform.
2. You will love and respect each other in spite of your shortcomings.
3. You will continue to work for the success of the marriage.
4. Disagreements are normal and expected, but you keep working toward a meeting of minds.
5. This is an exclusive relationship. "Forsaking all others," the marriage comes first.

> **"'For this reason a man shall leave his father and**
> **mother and be joined to his wife, and the two**
> **shall become one flesh.'"**
> MATTHEW 19:5

6. You permanently commit yourselves to this marriage.

THE STARTING POINT

Perhaps you have not yet made such vows—or if you have, you have not taken them seriously. Either way, if you expect to make your marriage better, such a commitment is needed as a starting point. These Bible verses are similar to your marriage vows:

> **Fulfill my joy by being like-minded, having the same love, *being* of one accord, of one mind. *Let* nothing *be done* through selfish ambition or conceit, but in lowliness of mind let each esteem others better than himself. Let each of you look out not only for his own interests, but also for the interests of others.**
> PHILIPPIANS 2:2–4

Here's what these verses say:

1. You intend to come to a meeting of minds.
2. You consider your partner as important as yourself.
3. You intend to look out for your partner's interests as well as your own.

Doesn't that sound great? Such a foundation must exist to succeed. There is more:

> **Let this mind be in you which was also in Christ Jesus, who, being in the form of God, did not consider it robbery to be equal with God, but made Himself of no reputation, taking the form of a servant, *and* coming in the likeness of men. And being found in appearance as a man, He humbled Himself and became obedient to *the point of* death, even the death of the cross.**
> PHILIPPIANS 2:5–8

What do these verses say?

1. You intend to serve one another.
2. Both partners will comply with decisions made by the partnership (obedience). That is being subject to each other in the fear of Christ. That is cooperation.

3. You are quite capable of going it alone. You choose to submit to the partnership until death.

BUILDING ON YOUR COMMITMENT—DECIDING ON THE GUIDELINES

In marriage, like playing doubles in tennis, each partner must make many independent decisions. So the first and most difficult decisions facing a newly married couple involve dividing up responsibilities and setting up guidelines and rules that will help you make mutually agreeable decisions as you act independently.

The need for new guidelines, or revising the ones you have set up, will gradually unfold as weeks and months go by. This means many little meetings together, called by either one of you, as the need arises.

CAUTION!

1. Decision making is the name of the game.
2. There will be intelligent decisions and dumb ones.
3. To make the best possible decisions, both partners must lay their likes, dislikes, ambitions, goals, interests, abilities, and thoughts on the table.
4. The meetings must be regular, whether formal or informal.
5. Generalizations or statistics about what "men" are like or what "women" are like will not serve you here.
6. It is important for you to know what your partner is like.

WARNING!

Some people are reluctant to disrobe and reveal their bodies in front of their partners. It is even more difficult to disrobe mentally and emotionally before your partner. You do not want to offend or reveal ideas and thoughts that might be held against you. Also, you might not be able to handle what your partner reveals.

I am not suggesting that this process will be easy or completed in an evening. There will be surprises—and delays—in deciding. Read the list again: likes, dislikes, ambitions, goals, interests, abilities, thoughts. These gradually unfold over months, even years. And they will change.

Promises, commitments, and agreements made today may not make sense at all next year or next month. Decision making is a process that goes on and on as long as we live.

AS CHRIST LOVED . . .

So the husband has the last word. He can break those unresolved deadlocks, but it must be done in love. Being the head is much more than resolving deadlocks.

> **For the husband is head of the wife, as also Christ is head of the church; and He is the Savior of the body.**
> EPHESIANS 5:23

What did Christ have to do? What was His mission to the church? He described it this way:

> **"For I have not spoken on My own *authority*; but the Father who sent Me gave Me a command, what I should say and what I should speak. And I know that His command is everlasting life. Therefore, whatever I speak, just as the Father has told Me, so I speak."**
> JOHN 12:49–50

Jesus was bound by His Father's words. What His Father had commanded leads us to eternal life. You cannot have better instructions than those.

A commandment comes to mind that will give a married couple a lifetime challenge:

. . . submitting to one another in the fear of God.
EPHESIANS 5:21

A man and woman earnestly search the Bible for guidelines and diligently develop a working plan so the marriage will last until "death do us part." The husband leads the way in doing this and making the marriage better.

WHAT JESUS DID AS THE HEAD

Jesus had commandments from God that would lead us to eternal life. The Gospels show how He went about getting these commandments across to the people. He
- taught
- discussed
- reasoned
- meditated
- suffered aggression
- dealt with challenges to His authority
- lectured
- warned
- overruled
- rebuked
- dealt with burdens and sickness
- resisted injustice
- expected loyalty
- moved aggressively

HOW PEOPLE RESPONDED

The people responded by—following, obeying, worshiping, being astonished and angry, arguing, resisting, betraying, and abandoning Him. It is said of Jesus:

He came to His own, and His own did not receive Him.
JOHN 1:11

**But God demonstrates His own love toward us, in
that while we were still sinners, Christ died for us.**
ROMANS 5:8

Notice, the people are rejecting Jesus, who loved them and died to give them eternal life. Yet Jesus devoted His life to the church, even though many refused to follow Him.

It is my observation that we may resist any rule, however beneficial, that gets in our way. The drive to go our own way is not corrected by a set of rules, not even if someone dies to defend them, as Jesus did.

THE PRICE OF HEADSHIP

If a husband's responsibility to his wife is the same as Christ's to the Church, he must

1. take the lead in determining the guidelines that assure the eternal life of the marriage; and
2. work at carrying them out until death, whatever the resistance.

MARRIAGE: A FORTY-YEAR HAUL, MAYBE EVEN FIFTY OR SIXTY

This is what Jesus said about leadership:

**"And whoever of you desires to be first shall be
slave of all."**
MARK 10:44

What then is expected of the husband? He is to be a lifetime slave to the task of making the marriage work. Many a man gets a cold shoulder when he comes home. He cannot count on his wife to carry out the rules.

You might say she sins against the marriage. Still, he hangs in there until he dies.

Granted, men sin against the marriage, too. Leaders often do a lousy job. In that case, the wife hangs in for a lifetime.

You do not dump a business because you made some bad decisions. It may take a few years of blood, sweat, and tears to correct mistakes.

Marriage is a forty-year haul. There may be some bad years. You may even pile poor decisions upon poor decisions. But you stick it out. How is this possible?

Only if God's love bathes your heart. Marriage is more than a ceremony. It is hard work, sacrifice, and effort as you yield yourself to God's love. Because you yield yourself to God's love does not mean your partner will do so. To yield to God is a personal choice for each partner.

WHEN YOU MAKE A BAD DECISION

Most marriages have their sore spots. I think of a couple who bought a home far beyond their means. The husband yielded to his wife's pressure to buy it after resisting for several years. Both soon agreed it was a mistake. Prices dropped, so they were stuck with it.

A bad decision. But both partners are working shoulder to shoulder to make the best of it. It may take years to get out from under this burden. No use jumping on her. The husband made the final decision. They were both wrong.

Another couple bought a house beyond their means. In this case, the husband purchased it in spite of his wife's protests. He told her he was the head of the house and she was out of line sticking her nose into his business. She had no choice but to concede.

The decision was a bad one. His hopes for making large sums of money did not materialize. Now they have a heavy burden she did not want in the first place. She was right. He was wrong. But they are working shoulder to shoulder to make the best of it.

We see another couple—in their early twenties, married three years. She has never learned to cook or keep house. To this day, their house is a shambles. At mealtime, they either eat out or each ferrets something out of the refrigerator. Neither knows any better. They live like two sloppy roommates. Tensions are growing between them.

Under these conditions, he is still the head. He needs to be coached step by step like the man-child he is. He gets no cooperation from his wife. The marriage is dying, but it does not have to. He can and is hanging in there, learning about the Christian life and leadership as fast as he can.

With patience, endurance, and hard work, he may yet save his marriage. He is staking his life on it. Is his wife persuaded to change because he is working on becoming a better leader? Not yet.

BLUEPRINT FROM GOD

Husbands do have some orders on what their attitudes toward their wives should be:

> For the husband is head of the wife, as also Christ is head of the church; and He is the Savior of the body. Therefore, just as the church is subject to Christ, so *let* the wives *be* to their own husbands in everything.
>
> Husbands, love your wives, just as Christ also loved the church and gave Himself for it, that He might sanctify and cleanse it with the washing of water by the word, that He might present it to Himself a glorious church, not having spot or wrinkle or any such thing, but that it should be holy and without blemish. So husbands ought to love their own wives as their own bodies; he who loves his wife loves himself. For no one ever hated his own flesh, but nourishes and cherishes it, just as the Lord *does* the church. For we are members of His body, of His flesh and of His bones. "For this reason a man shall leave his father and mother and be joined to his wife, and the two

shall become one flesh." This is a great mystery, but I speak concerning Christ and the church. Nevertheless let each one of you in particular so love his own wife as himself, and let the wife *see* that she respects *her* husband.

EPHESIANS 5:23–33

Let us examine a few high spots of these verses.

A LOVE THAT WILL NOT QUIT

Husbands, love your wives, just as Christ also
loved the church and gave Himself for it.
EPHESIANS 5:25

Your wife cannot stop you from loving her. if you draw your love from God. The kind of love you need is described in 1 Corinthians 13:4–8.

Your love for your wife has nothing to do with her choices. Your love involves yielding yourself to God.

Now hope does not disappoint, because the love
of God has been poured out in our hearts by the
Holy Spirit who was given to us.
ROMANS 5:5

A GOAL THAT WILL NOT QUIT

. . . that He might present it to Himself a glorious
church, not having spot or wrinkle or any such
thing, but that it should be holy and without
blemish.
EPHESIANS 5:27

This verse implies that you keep trying to help your wife become the finest person possible. If she rejects your efforts, back off for a while, even for a few years. Here is more advice to husbands:

> **Likewise, *you* husbands, dwell with *them* with**
> **understanding, giving honor to the wife, as to the**
> **weaker vessel, and as *being* heirs together of the**
> **grace of life, that your prayers may not be hindered.**
> 1 PETER 3:7

Yes, let the husband get to know his wife, honor her, and treat her as he would a rare, precious, delicate vase, even if she tells him to get lost. The husband's purpose for his wife should be the same as Christ's purpose for the church. Together they work toward blending two lives into one. Even as the Lord Jesus gives commands that are in the best interests of His followers, so the husband must make decisions in the best interests of the family.

A young couple stopped to visit some friends while returning home from a distant state. They intended to visit briefly and go on. Their friends invited them to stay for supper. The wife wanted to stay. The husband, thinking of responsibilities facing both of them the next day, turned down the invitation. The wife was unhappy about the decision. Later, as they arrived home at a reasonable hour and had a good rest, both agreed that his decision was best.

Thus, the husband who is following after the Lord is living and thinking according to His will. He will take leadership as the head of the wife, even in the face of resistance. The Bible has some specific commands to the husband:

> **Husbands, love your wives, just as Christ also**
> **loved the church and gave Himself for it.**
> EPHESIANS 5:25

> So husbands ought to love their own wives as
> their own bodies; he who loves his wife loves
> himself. . . . "For this reason a man shall leave his
> father and mother and be joined to his wife, and
> the two shall become one flesh."
> EPHESIANS 5:28A, 31

> Likewise, *you* husbands, dwell with *them* with
> understanding, giving honor to the wife, as to the
> weaker vessel, and as *being* heirs together of the
> grace of life, that your prayers may not be hindered.
> 1 PETER 3:7

> Husbands, love your wives and do not be bitter
> toward them.
> COLOSSIANS 3:19

For a husband to love his wife as Christ loves the church is a miracle, for He came not to be served, but to serve. A Christian husband ought not to have the attitude that he deserves service, but rather that he enjoys the privilege of serving. Christ gave His life for His church. The charge that God gives to a husband is to be dedicated to his wife and family even unto death. You are to give yourself faithfully to seek her well-being.

If wives are to submit to the leadership of their husbands, every husband has the responsibility of being the kind of man who warrants submission.

Together they seek to experience the reality of what the Word of God teaches about their daily life together. The Lord Jesus said, "Love your neighbor as yourself." Paul said something very much like that:

> So husbands ought to love their own wives as their
> own bodies; he who loves his wife loves himself.
> EPHESIANS 5:28

The husband needs to be truly loving and diligently searching out ways to help his wife become the finest person she could possibly be. Usually it is the other way around. The husband is bitter, hostile, and has quit trying. He is preoccupied with himself and filled with self-pity. He thinks about getting even, rather than healing the marriage. These attitudes cause marriages to collapse.

How long do you endure? Until death. That is what Jesus did.

LOVE HER AS YOU LOVE YOURSELF

So husbands ought to love their own wives as their own bodies; he who loves his wife loves himself.
EPHESIANS 5:28

I once had an experience that showed me how much I loved my own body. I dropped something on my little toe, which, until then, I had hardly noticed. Suddenly, my toe was the center of attention. I bathed it, wrapped it, favored it, even changed my way of walking for the sake of that toe. When your body is healthy, you are hardly aware of its parts. Let one part get hurt, and it demands your attention.

Your marriage is like that. Without conflicts, you are hardly aware of attitudes or rules. When there is a conflict, it demands your attention. When your wife is hurting, when there is strain or tension, it is a signal for your individual attention. You take the initiative. This is no simple matter if your efforts are resisted.

Your wife is entitled to this kind of dedication. She can call problems to your attention, can express her views, make recommendations, and have them taken seriously. She has half interest in this partnership. You have left father and mother and have become one. Your goal is to become so committed to each other that you respond as one person, rather than two.

THE HUSBAND'S TOP PRIORITY

If I understand the Bible, the husband's top priority is his wife—not his work, not his recreation, not his children, but his wife!

If a husband understands this, he tries to use all the talent and ability of both partners. He is responsible for harmonious relationships. He has enough meetings with his wife to make sure the duties of the partnership are carried out. This takes the best daily and weekly efforts until "death do us part."

That is some assignment. The divorce rate would drop dramatically if we men held up our end of our marriage.

SOUND A LITTLE BETTER?

How is that? This is God's plan for managing a marriage. There is submission on the part of both parties.

- First, husband and wife agree to develop and maintain a plan that both will support.
- Second, the wife submits to her husband's judgments when there is a deadlock.
- Third, the husband submits to the responsibility of making the plan work. That is leadership.

CHAPTER 8

One Flesh,
One Mind

A married couple told me this story. I will call him Brad and her Sally. The decision to yield their lives to the Lord was postponed again and again because, to them, becoming a Christian meant giving up a lifestyle that gave them much satisfaction. They believed that life would be dull, uninteresting, and frustrating without these pleasures.

Gradually the way of life that they were clinging to was becoming more and more burdensome. They wandered into a church one Sunday and responded to the pastor's invitation to ask the Lord to come into their lives. Then they decided to explore the Bible for direction into a fulfilling life. They found some strange sayings. As they put them into practice, they experienced joyful contentment that made the old way of life drab in comparison. There was nothing to give up. There was a far better life to take up.

The first principle that caught their attention was Jesus teaching His disciples:

"For even the Son of Man did not come to be
served, but to serve, and to give His life a ransom
for many."
Mark 10:45

They thought that the ultimate in Christian living is to be served. Their idea of first-class living was taking a vacation at a resort where everything was done for them.

As Sally thought more about this verse, she had to face some truths. She was becoming more and more aware of Brad's tendency to look out for himself and ignore her needs. He was coming to the same conclusion about her. They were beginning to nurse a growing and unspoken grudge against each other. For example, when she came home after grocery shopping, he used to come to the car to greet her and carry the groceries into the house. Gradually, his greeting shifted to when she came into the house. It seemed to her that he reluctantly went out to bring in the groceries.

To move from avoiding being helpful to being willing to help each other has changed their relationship from boredom to kindness.

Jesus taught another principle that puzzled them, but made sense the more they thought about it.

"Therefore, whatever you want men to do to you,
do also to them . . ."
Matthew 7:12

They found another verse:

". . . You shall love your neighbor as yourself."
Matthew 22:39

Jesus is saying that you can be as good to yourself as you wish. Whatever you expect to be done on your behalf is the way you should treat others. Such behavior toward others is reverse selfishness.

They found another verse that made them think:

> **. . . submitting to one another in the fear of God.**
> EPHESIANS 5:21

This verse caused them to recall the days when they were dating. One of their favorite pastimes was to swing and sway on roller skates in tune with the music. They were not responding in unison to some of the music that they were facing now.

As Brad and Sally started ordering their lives in tune with biblical principles, they began to experience a joyful contentment that they had never experienced. This is the experience of a couple who initially resisted anything to do with the Bible. Then they chose to order their lives by what they found in the Bible. They found the key was becoming like-minded.

GUIDELINES

Guidelines can be resisted or embraced. One principle that leads to a contented married life sounds like doomsday to people who cherish their independence:

> **But I want you to know that the head of every man is Christ, the head of woman *is* man, and the head of Christ *is* God.**
> 1 CORINTHIANS 11:3

If we teach that the husband is the head of the wife, we must equally stress its counterpart, that Christ is the head of the husband. If the husband follows after Christ, then his leadership of his wife must be like Christ's leadership of man. He gave His life for the church. A husband gives his life for his wife. Did you feel yourself stiffening up a bit when you read that verse?

HER JUDGMENT

In marriage, the wife has a half interest in the partnership. Her stake is equal to her husband's. Her judgment and experience are needed to make many of the decisions. She should be expected to do all she can to influence the direction of the partnership, to participate vigorously in the decision-making process.

If she disagrees with her husband's views, she should say so. He should know whether or not she has changed her mind. And she needs to know what is on her husband's mind. Together, a couple works at finding a mutually agreeable decision.

Agreement on a family plan (not "Joe's plan" or "Mary's plan") is where cooperation begins. Then it takes daily effort, constant examination, and frequent changes to keep it going.

For example, after making a sincere effort to please your partner, you announce that you do not really like what you are doing.

"Yeah, I went with you to a few concerts when we were dating, but I do not really like concerts."

"You do not like concerts?"

Or, "Well, I went with you to those basketball games when we were dating, but I really do not get excited about sports."

"What? Run that by me again."

Your partner might suddenly announce he or she does not enjoy going to church, wants to change jobs, or would like to move from the area. Anything might come up.

Take the warning. This process of decision making can be risky and explosive. From what is on the table—the information about yourselves and the decisions to be made—you forget mutually agreed-upon choices. But deadlocks will come when your best efforts end up in disagreement. It is the husband's responsibility to settle a deadlocked issue.

What could be more fun than two people who care about each other and want to please each other planning for the future?

And remember, all in the presence of God.

Without God's love and a sincere desire to consider the interests of your partner, decision making becomes intolerable. With God's love you can build on a foundation of commitment and develop the best plan possible for this most important partnership.

THE AGENDA

You cannot cover everything in one evening. Some decisions involve more discussion than you thought they needed. Others might have to wait for another day. Few decisions must be made today. Agree on a time limit for discussing difficult problems.

You divide responsibilities according to ability, interests, likes and dislikes. Who will handle the fundraising? The purchasing? The accounting? The cooking? Who will make decisions in case of a deadlock?

You may have taken a responsibility your partner could have done better or easier. So you negotiate a swap. Each partner must handle some responsibilities that cannot be exchanged, whether you like them or not. Then there are decisions about church, social life, in-laws.

We are talking about continuous, ongoing meetings, necessary because of constant changes. For instance:

- He had accepted the bookkeeping job, but she can do it more accurately and quickly, so she took that one.
- He originally agreed to go shopping with his wife. After a while they scrapped that idea because she did not really need his company while shopping.

Agreements and assigned responsibilities are not cast in concrete. They can be changed. Responsibilities should not be like this: "You promised me two years ago, and I am holding you to it for life."

In a business, partners develop policies, procedures, and rules. They make changes necessary to accomplish the objectives of the business. They observe how responsibility and authority are handled, and determine if everyone is well placed. They even note who can take on more responsibility.

Marriage involves the same process. Both partners must be actively involved. Discussions may take place while driving in the car, sitting at the kitchen table, in the living room or bedroom, on the patio—anywhere.

In a nutshell, both husband and wife should be expected to participate vigorously and forthrightly in the search for mutually agreeable decisions.

That is submission.

CAUSE FOR DISORDER

Remember, the discussion goes on in the atmosphere of the love of God. If this spirit is missing in either partner, then table the issue and get your hearts straightened out. Your attitude is a personal matter between you and God. You can come back to the issue another day. A key Bible verse is important here:

> For where envy and self-seeking *exist,* confusion
> and every evil thing *will be* there.
>
> JAMES 3:16

BACK TO THE ISSUE

You need to come back to the issue when you have tabled a decision. Do not let it fester too long. Once you are filled with the love of God, you can review the facts of the tabled item and settle it. Your marriage is too important to be making decisions without the love of God in your heart.

Love bears and endures all things. An unresolved issue or decision different from yours does not separate you from the love of God.

After all, you should not be expected to pretend agreement if your judgment differs from your partner's. He should have the benefit of her opinion, and she needs his.

Remember the truth expressed in God's word to Israel:

If you are willing and obedient,
You shall eat the good of the land.
ISAIAH 1:19

Obedience is not enough. Submitting to your husband means willingly submitting also to the responsibilities of keeping a home—not resignation, but submission.

SUBMISSION TO OLDER WOMEN

One of the tasks given to "aged women" is that of teaching.

. . . that they admonish the young women to love their
husbands, to love their children, to be discreet, chaste,
homemakers, good, obedient to their own husbands,
that the word of God may not be blasphemed.
TITUS 2:4–5

Here is a new career to master. Paul suggests that the wife should look to older, more experienced women for training. This is a wholesome concept. Most big businesses pass knowledge gained from many years of service down from older, experienced employees to new, inexperienced employees. In this way, the best methods are preserved. This again implies submission. It implies the willingness to learn from others. This idea goes counter to much modern-day thinking—that older people have nothing to contribute to the younger generation. To give proper honor and appreciation to the older women and to be willing to learn from them would save untold heartaches for many young women.

THE PROPER SPIRIT

. . . that they admonish the young women to love
their husbands, to love their children . . .
TITUS 2:4

One of the great privileges of a wife is that of loving her husband and her children. This love is not stimulated by the husband or children alone but must first come from God and go out to them. What is meant by love? It is not hugs and kisses. It is not passion. You need not be married to find someone who can arouse passion within you. On the other hand, a husband and wife can embrace each other, and yet each knows that there is a barrier between them. An invisible but very real wall can separate husband, wife, and children. This is well expressed by a popular song:

> There is a wall between us;
> It's not made of stone:
> The more we are together,
> The more I am alone.

It is Christian love that binds—gentleness, kindness, goodness, patience, longsuffering, compassion, temperance.

Many people say, "If you treat me well, I will treat you well. The responsibility is on you." Being good or bad does not lie with someone else! It is a decision for you to make. This is a struggle. You often must struggle with the decision to ask God for love that you can bestow upon a husband or a child, who may not return it. You can submit to your marriage with a stony heart or with a loving heart.

A KEEPER AT HOME

To be a keeper at home is a high calling (Titus 2:4–5). Wise purchasing, wise planning, and creating a wholesome atmosphere in the home require the best that is in you.

It is a fortunate man who finds a woman who will dedicate herself to keeping the home and maintaining a happy relationship with her children and her husband. For a woman to give herself to her family is a high calling indeed. Essentially, our Lord poured His life into only twelve men.

I was a Sunday school teacher for a newlywed class. One of the couples, Dick and Kay, decided to build a Christian home and she would be the homemaker.

It is March 1995. We are sitting in Dick and Kay Erb's family room on the side of a mountain. There is a spectacular view of Colorado Springs from the porch facing east. To the north is a view of Pike's Peak.

Dick is an executive with Focus on the Family. He supervised their move from California to Colorado Springs and then the construction of their new campus.

I was Kay's Sunday school teacher in 1965. She was the new music teacher in a Flint, Michigan, school. When she sat down to play the piano in the church auditorium, it was obvious who the church pianist would be. She was in her place in the Sunday school each week. When the class had a get-together, she was the one who did the decorating and anything else that was needed.

Dick, a local, goal-oriented young man, showed up in the class. He had three goals in mind—graduate from college, find a challenging job, and establish a Christian home.

It was love at first sight, or close to it, when he met Kay. They married in 1968. He was twenty-five, she was twenty-three.

He sang in the choir and taught Sunday school. Dick had recently graduated from General Motors Institute with an engineering degree. They offered him a challenging job in management, which he accepted. Two goals down and one to go. Dick and Kay were married in 1968 and started to build a Christian home—the start of goal number three. They have been at it for thirty-one years.

Kay taught music until it was close to time to deliver their first child. Jerri was born ten months after they married. Kay resigned her school teaching job to become a homemaker. Steve was born in February 1971, Lauri in September 1972, and Dan was born in 1973. A major part of her time for the next twenty-five years was invested in guiding those children into mature adulthood.

Commitment is a key word to describe them as they proceeded to build a Christian family.

Kay always had multiple interests. A major activity was using her artistry at the piano. She would have between fifteen and forty piano students. Crafts, sewing, and decorating occupied her spare moments. Reading the Bible, prayer, and ladies meetings rounded out her interests. Kay insists that never in her married life was she bored or unfulfilled. She never looked back. Her only frustration was that she had too much to do.

Dick was a management trainee with the Buick division of General Motors. He moved one step up the ladder every eighteen months, achieving a job title of chief engineer of all tooling.

Dick began to notice that the demands of the job required increasing amounts of time and concentration. To climb any higher would require making the job his life. The demands did not fit his goal of building a Christian home and being active in church.

I was still their Sunday school teacher. Each Sunday the emphasis was on building a personal spiritual life, a Christian home, and serving the Lord. My own career was developing as a counselor and international speaker under the watchful eyes of the class. When I was away, Mel and Berthan Willott taught the class. Berthan and Eva, my wife, modeled the Spirit-filled homemaker for the class. Mel and I attempted the role of modeling the Spirit-filled husband and father.

I watched Dick and Kay attempt to keep a balance between a wholesome personal life, work, church, and home. Something had to give.

I had purchased an ice cream parlor franchise. At the time, I had one in operation and it was losing money. Dick shared his concern with me about living a balanced Christian life. To make a long story short, we prayerfully decided that he would leave General Motors and use his management skills to build my franchise. When we sold the chain of seven ice cream parlors six years later, it was with gratitude to God for a successful adventure. We kept a reasonable balance between work, church, home, and personal life.

We sold to a large hotel and restaurant group. Dick moved to an executive position with them.

Four years later Dick shared with me that he was again at a cross-roads. He was offered a major management position that would demand too much of his time and a move that was not in the best interest of the family. I was involved in another business venture at the time. He joined us. That venture ended up in a huge loss for both of us.

Life has its ups and downs. The lesson we learned out of a long association is this:

> **I have learned to be content, whatever the circumstances may be. I know now how to live when things are difficult and I know how to live when things are prosperous. In general and in particular I have learned the secret of facing either plenty or poverty.**
> PHILIPPIANS 4:11–12, PHILLIPS

> **My God will supply all that you need from his glorious resources in Christ Jesus.**
> PHILIPPIANS 4:19, PHILLIPS

To date Dick and Kay are working on keeping a balanced life in an empty nest. There are ten grandchildren. Kay is back at work, the gracious hostess who greets you when you visit Focus on the Family.

One of the key commitments that Dick and Kay made as they began their journey together: They would be unyielding if one of them considered any involvement that would hinder the balance between a Christian home, personal life, work, and church.

THE PROPER ADORNING

Peter speaks of a quality in a wife that is of great worth in the sight of God. He speaks of this with reference to a wife whose husband does not obey the Word. However, any wife will do well to live by this exhortation in 1 Peter 3:1–4. In these days there is much emphasis upon outward appearance. Women spend a great deal of time and money on clothes, jewelry, care of the complexion, and hair. Women should look just as lovely as they possibly can. The intent of this passage, however, is to stress the truth that these outward things are not the ornaments that are of God. This is the ornament that counts:

> . . . rather *let it be* the hidden person of the heart,
> with the incorruptible *beauty* of a gentle and quiet
> spirit, which is very precious in the sight of God.
> 1 PETER 3:4

You should look as attractive as you can. In addition, and more important, is a meek and quiet spirit that shines through your face, gets into your muscles, into your nervous system, and into your heart. Why? For your own good, of course. For your own happiness, of course. But just as important is your influence on your husband and the atmosphere that you create for the people in your life. A meek and quiet spirit that dominates your life is one of the greatest accomplishments possible for a wife. In the sight of God it is of great worth. Such a spirit will win the man who does not obey the Word.

A lady told of this incident: Her husband came home late from work because he stopped on the way home to play golf. She resented this very much and was seething within when he came home. After supper he announced, "Honey, we are going out for a ride. I have a surprise for you." She did not want to go anywhere because she wanted to nurse her grievance. He insisted. They stopped in front of a pet shop. He went in and came out with a particular parakeet that she had been noticing and had said she would like to have. She tried to look grateful, but within she was very much ashamed.

The parakeet is now at home; but she doesn't enjoy it because it represents to her a symbol of a seething heart, rather than a gift received with a meek and quiet spirit. This woman is a Christian. Her husband, who is not, treats her better than she treats him. If she wants to influence him for Christ, she must avail herself of the proper equipment—a meek and quiet spirit. Then the Word of God will not be blasphemed.

In these days there are many tottering, weak, unhappy marriages. Could it be that the key to strengthening many of them is in the hands of the wife? This passage from 1 Peter would say so. Wives have a high calling, a great job to be done. The proper dress for the job is spiritual and invisible. It is available only from God—the adornment of a meek and quiet spirit. With God's help the wife can provide the haven that her husband and children need in these tense days.

THOSE TWO-TONED SHOES

Without guidelines and the love of God in your hearts, you become candidates for the consulting room. That is where I met Lars and Carol. Lars was an impressive man. And did he ever have a beautiful wife!

She was gorgeous. You looked at her and said, "Wow!"

And that's what I was thinking to myself when I suddenly did a double take. Could this really be true? Sure enough, this lovely lass had a black eye.

Lars had done it.

It had all started one Thursday. Lars woke up in an ugly mood. Mind you, this man was a college graduate and had a good job. The family lived in a fine house and went to church every week. Yet, that Thursday, Lars woke up in an ugly mood. How come?

His explanation: "I am like that."

He assumed that if you are like that, there was nothing you could do about it—certainly not change.

Lars and Carol had been married long enough to have four children. Lars knew Carol was going downtown that day to buy shoes, so he made a little speech at breakfast.

"Now, listen here," he said, glaring at his wife, "I want you to get something straight! I know you are going downtown today to buy shoes.

I do not mind you buying black shoes, brown shoes, even white shoes, but I do not want you coming home with any two-toned shoes, do you understand?"

Carol had made up her mind what she would do, before Lars got halfway through that speech. She was already thinking, *So help me, I am going downtown and coming home with four pairs of two-toned shoes.* She had not intended to do that, but his speech made her angry and rebellious. Her logic was that any woman who got talked to like Lars had talked to her was not responsible for her decisions.

Would you buy that idea?

By now, I suppose most of our readers have taken sides.

Well, she bought the shoes, came home, caught the kids, and put the shoes on them. By the time Lars came home that evening, those shoes had three hours of wear. They were used shoes.

She won round two.

Round three was coming—three days later. And, believe it or not, Lars (remember, a college graduate, nice big house, good job, and all) again woke up in an ugly mood.

On a Sunday morning! Could you believe it?

That was bad enough, but another drama was about to unfold. His gorgeous wife had pulled four pairs of two-toned shoes out of their respective closets and put them in the basement, where every Sunday morning it was dad's responsibility to shine them.

So Lars went down to the basement, in an ugly mood.

And things got uglier.

Imagine the scene. An angry father was facing four scuffed-up pairs of two-toned shoes.

He glared at them. Then he started polishing them. Can you predict what kind of a job he did on them?

Sure enough, he got some black on the white of the first shoe. When he was finished with the first pair of shoes, he gave them to the rightful owner. The child ran up the stairs, and Carol's reaction to Lars' efforts echoed down the stairs.

"Is that the best your father can do?"

Try to picture him now. He grits his teeth and finishes the second and third pairs. Now three children have shoes polished. But Carol notices one shoeless child.

Downstairs, a very angry dad is working on the fourth pair of shoes when his wife's voice comes downstairs again.

"Is your father finished yet?"

Bingo! He starts polishing with vengeance. He finishes the fourth pair and stomps up the stairs. At the head of the stairs stands his wife, looking down her nose at him.

Can you see her? Defiant. Resolute. Every inch of her body taking him on. She fires out at him, a nasty glint in her eye, "About time!"

And that is when he let her have it. Right in the eye. Have you ever done that? Let me ask you men another question. Have you ever considered doing it? Some of you ladies may not know how close you have come to that black eye.

Well, Lars had not done this before either. There is always a first time for everything, and what Lars did was to send his wife sprawling on the kitchen floor. At least he helped her up. And they finally agreed on something—that she had a black eye.

They were two shocked people as they told me their story. What was wrong?

1. The love of God was missing.
2. They had no guidelines.
3. They were not committed to cooperation.

Lars was a hostile, self-seeking man. When he lashed out angrily at Carol, he got her fighting mad and rebellious. They were opponents, not teammates. All these years, decision making was a contest. When he won, she lost. If she won, he lost.

When I pointed this out to them, they agreed on something else: they were both angry at me.

As we noted earlier, marriage can magnify, rather than eliminate, your sins. What were Lars' and Carol's sins? Hostility, self-seeking, and rebellion.

But people cool off. So did Lars and Carol. Later, they recalled my little speech and admitted it was true. They did repent, became children of God, and let Him bathe their hearts with His love.

FAMILY CONFERENCES

Across the years, there will be many conferences. Either partner can call the meeting for any of these reasons:
1. To set a policy or a rule
2. To make some changes
3. To report a problem
4. To report on progress
5. Because one is not carrying out his or her responsibility
6. To express praise and admiration for a partner's performance

A biblical marriage makes no allowance for independence. Rather, the husband and wife give themselves completely and continuously to their duties and responsibilities, each contributing what he can to a single whole. After all, God said the two people of a marriage are to become one flesh. And surely if one flesh, one mind.

CHAPTER 9

The Tiebreaker

Wives, submit to your own husbands as to the Lord.
EPHESIANS 5:22

Ouch! There it is. The most hotly debated Bible verse concerning marriage. "Why should the wife do all the submitting?" That is the hot question. She does not have to. This verse does not stand alone. Remember the one before it?

> **. . . submitting to one another in the fear of God.**
> EPHESIANS 5:21

And another:

> **Let each of you look out not only for his own
> interests, but also for the interests of others.**
> PHILIPPIANS 2:4

The matter of submission arises when opinions differ over a decision even with all the facts on the table. The only solution is to submit to the judgment of a tiebreaker.

IT HAPPENS IN BUSINESS

Tom and Dennis had been friends for years. Both were computer wizards and had held executive positions. Across the years, they talked often about their work and developed respect and admiration for each other. Both had saved large sums of their huge salaries. They pooled their savings and purchased a consulting company, which provided computer training and assessment for large corporations—a dream come true.

Now these fine, experienced, Christian gentlemen could pool their knowledge. It would be great fun to work as equal partners. They had a nice, new building with an expensive conference room. Here they came for their idea sessions.

Soon they realized they had some acute problems. They differed about handling employees. They were having trouble dividing up the responsibilities, and neither knew enough about accounting.

Their fancy conference room could not solve their problems. Even friendship, knowledge, experience, and dedication were not enough to settle the differences.

Most of their problems resulted from having done things differently—and successfully—for years. Tom was used to giving instructions and expecting them to be carried out. He had been the boss. So had Dennis. Now they were partners—with brilliant, but differing ideas. It was not a matter of right or wrong.

They were able to discuss their differences. They clearly defined and understood each other's viewpoints. But they deadlocked when it came to making decisions. Honesty, understanding, respect, knowledge, and experience did not settle the deadlocks. The theory that two friendly partners can each do their own thing was not working.

They were frustrated and disgusted. They had even had a few shouting matches, with both of them storming angrily out of their beautiful conference room—and ultimately into a consulting room.

THE BASIC PROBLEM

We agreed there were two basic problems: (1) each turned to his own way (self-seeking) and (2) both needed God's love.

Sound familiar? So what should they do? Repent, asking God to forgive and bathe their hearts with His love. They needed a love that is patient, does not seek its own, is not provoked, and rejoices in the truth.

THE SPECIFIC PROBLEM

Tom and Dennis did this, but they still needed to resolve their differences. They went to an outside consultant who really dropped a bombshell: they must choose a president who would then settle the disagreements.

But . . . but . . . we are equal partners.

"True. There is just no other way, however, to solve your disagreements. You also need outside help with your accounting."

A bitter pill to swallow, but it was either follow the advice or lose the business.

After weeks of agonizing, they chose Dennis to be the president. They spent the next months dividing up responsibilities and developing policies and procedures both of them could live with.

Let us take a brief look at some of those conference room discussions. Both men preferred managing the sales, neither one wanted advertising, purchasing, or supervising the office staff. But all the work had to be done. Without going into great detail, here is how they distributed some of the duties:

1. Tom managed the office, personnel relations, and maintenance.
2. Dennis got sales, advertising, and engineering.
3. They divided purchasing. Tom made the purchases for the office; Dennis for external needs. Tom became technical director.

A POINT TO REMEMBER

They were still equal partners, both vitally interested in all areas of the business. They consulted each other, reviewed any decisions they wished to, and participated equally in making them.

Tom had the last word in the office with Dennis contributing his knowledge occasionally. In the field, Dennis made the decisions with Tom contributing his knowledge occasionally.

However, Dennis, as president, had the last word in any decision. Rarely did he overrule Tom, but it did happen occasionally. They once were deadlocked over whether to buy a new or used computer. It almost killed Dennis to overrule his knowledgeable friend, but there was no other way. They could not argue endlessly over a machine.

The business grew and prospered. Tom and Dennis enjoyed working together. They learned to know each other better and developed confidence in each other's decision-making ability—a process that took many months.

As Tom and Dennis reviewed their rocky beginning, both admitted they had been vaguely aware that the question of the last word would have to be settled. They had pushed the question out of their thinking, hoping it would go away. They both wanted to be president, but their pride made it impossible for them to make the selection.

MANAGING YOUR MARRIAGE

Let us switch from Tom and Dennis to your marriage.

You are equal partners making decisions in marriage. Responsibilities must be divided up. You need policies, procedures, and rules in order to work cooperatively as well as independently.

There are some mothers who could not possibly take on any additional family responsibilities. Then there are those moms who breeze through the chores at home and are ready for something else by 10:00 every morning. My first wife was that way.

When my wife and I first started in this business of raising a family, we got together and listed all of our responsibilities. (Notice I said our responsibilities, not my wife's responsibilities or my responsibilities.)

Just a few of the many we detailed were housecleaning, money management, cooking, writing, radio work, children, cleaning the yard, travel planning, running a business, raising money, and food purchasing.

Then we divvied them up. Eva got money management, travel agent, housecleaning, cooking, children, food purchasing, and a bunch more. I was assigned writing, radio work, cleaning the yard, running a business, and raising money. These were assignments on the basis of training, ability, interest, and necessity.

How we met the responsibilities was not the question. The assignment was simple: These were the responsibilities each of us was to carry out. If my wife decided to add responsibilities outside the home, fine. But she would have to figure out some way to carry out her primary tasks.

The same went for any other activities I took on. It was okay as long as I kept the primary activities going. Of course, they kept changing as the children grew and demands on our time changed.

In all our planning and assigning, we kept one thing in mind: That plan of ours had to be a family plan. We made sure to remember that it was a Brandt plan, not Henry's plan or Eva's plan. It was our plan, and we had to carry out our responsibilities.

If you are not effectively busy at home, the next time you have one of those business meetings between husband and wife, volunteer for some more work! It sure beats being bored.

Remember, you are equal partners. You are both vitally interested in all areas of the marriage. As in a business, both consult with each other and participate in making decisions and reviewing them.

The wife usually has the last word in her areas of responsibility. She is the decision maker; her husband, the resource person. In his area, the husband makes the decisions, and his wife contributes her knowledge. Mostly they work independently in their areas within mutually agreed upon guidelines. Remember the conditions that make submission to one another a pleasant experience?

- Good will and friendship
- Pleasant anticipation
- The will to play by the rules
- The will to choose a captain
- The will to develop teamwork

You will enjoy working together as you know each other better and gain confidence in each other's decision-making ability. Developing faith and trust takes many months. Forging a new way of life from your different backgrounds takes time and patience.

To illustrate how a husband and wife practice submission to one another and to the head, here are three decisions made at our house.

DECISION MAKING

Once, my wife and I decided to buy a stereo. It would be a pleasant feature in our home. So we went shopping together, happily expecting to make an easy choice. We looked at one for $70 and another for $700. One of us preferred the cheaper model; the other, the expensive one. We got so hung up on the decision, we tabled it until the next evening. It would be simple. The best viewpoint would win. So we did just that.

Ladies before gentlemen, so she went first. I could hardly believe her presentation. Jumbled. No logic. No substance. How could she present such a feeble point of view?

When my turn came, I was confident, thinking *She will be impressed with my presentation.* So I gave it. It was systematic. Considered all aspects. It was logical. Funny thing, though. She did not think so. My presentation did not convince her to change her point of view. We were deadlocked!

We were facing one of those situations in marriage where everything had been said that could be said. All the facts were in. Still, Eva and I were on opposite sides.

And it will happen to you. Regardless of how dedicated or friendly you are, there will be deadlocks like this in your marriage. It is a controversial issue, but it must be settled.

THE LAST WORD

Here comes the answer to how you settle a deadlock in marriage. There is only one way. The husband has the last word. He has two options:

1. Make the decision himself
2. Ask his wife to make it

I settled the stereo deadlock by making the decision on which model we bought.

It was a grave, serious moment when Eva and I were deadlocked. She was as committed to this marriage as I. She and I both wanted the best for the marriage. This was not the time to be selfish or ignore her judgment.

It took a few days to ponder the issues, but the responsibility for making the decision was mine. Soon we were past the decision and enjoyed years of pleasant listening.

THE KITCHEN EXPERT

Before we get too excited about the question of who has the last word, let us look at another decision.

We were moving into a new home and had to decide the layout and decor of the kitchen. We both agreed that I knew nothing about kitchens. Eva had been around them at least thirty-five years, and besides, she was the one who would use it.

Who do you think should have carried the ball on kitchen decisions? The answer was obvious—Eva. That is how it was. There was no deadlock or even any question. It was obvious she would have the final say. We had many discussions about how to do it, but in this case, she was the decision maker and had the last word. This is called delegation.

After all, she was the expert and the expert should make the decisions.

TIME TO COMPROMISE

We had something come up in our family that required many conferences between us. The children tossed in their opinions, too.

It had to do with buying a new couch. The one we had was an unsightly piece of furniture, really broken-down.

Although we had little money to spare, we did have just enough for a new couch. Eva and I were ready to buy one when a complication arose.

School let out for the year and the children, who ranged in age from ten to fourteen, wanted to accompany me on a speaking trip a month later to Boston.

Only one catch. We did not have enough money to go to Boston as a family and still buy a couch. It was one or the other. Which to do? We batted it around for a few weeks. I discussed it with Eva. Eva discussed it with the children. I discussed it with the children. We all discussed it together at meals.

Either way, the family would have to do without something. A couch or a trip. It was a tough decision. I found myself on both sides of the question. So did Eva and the children. We kept tabling the matter. Finally, there were only a few days left before we would have to leave on the trip.

One point kept coming up in all the discussions.

"Dad, I sort of like our couch even though it is all beat up," one of the children would invariably say.

And it was true. Even the gang from church seemed to enjoy the old couch. They would come in and throw their bodies into its beat-up frame without any reservation or worry of further damage.

"Well, I guess we have done OK with this couch up to this moment. Another year will not hurt us."

With that comment, I decided to take the family with me to Boston.

We came home, happy with the trip but still facing a decrepit, old couch. During the next year, all of us at one time or another wondered if we had made the right decision.

The couch was so bad that when we replaced it a year later, we called Goodwill Industries to come and take it away. And, you know, they turned it down. We had to take it to the dump ourselves.

Some seemingly easy decisions can become complicated. There are no clear-cut solutions. But when the decisions are made, the issues are settled. You go on from there.

BOTH BACK UP THE DECISION!

Whichever of the two ways the husband settles the deadlock at that point, both submit to the decision and do all in their power to make it work.

CHAPTER 10

Handling the Routines

Everyone has routines—regular, unvarying procedures repeated over and over, day after day. A newly married couple must develop routines for living together.

The doctor, dentist, lawyer, and counselor all face a daily schedule, office procedures, handling money, filling out forms—routines. Even if you live alone, you face routines.

I know a single woman whose day demands that she pay attention to a multitude of details. To start, she must get out of bed. This implies owning a bed, bed sheets, pillows, pillowcases, and blankets. It means changing sheets, washing, and storing all these articles. It also means having paid for, or being in the process of paying for, these items.

Preparation for going to work requires some bathroom equipment—soap, deodorants, perfumes, curlers, scissors, towels. Then there is clothing, which means more purchasing, cleaning, pressing, washing, storing, replacing, and adding.

Eating breakfast requires purchasing, storing, cooking, dishes, utensils, silverware, and washing. It also involves scheduling time.

Then she's off to work, which requires financing and maintaining a car, garage, and driveway.

Her job requires purchasing and maintaining some equipment, some study, and getting along with others.

After work, she likes to relax in her living room. This requires furniture, rugs, drapes, curtains, a television, a radio, and a newspaper. It involves cleaning house, washing windows, and furnishing heat or air-conditioning.

The house sits on a lot, which involves cutting grass and working on flower beds.

Then there is the evening. This may mean sports, restaurants, church, parties at her house or someone else's, and more clothes and equipment. Then it is bedtime and setting an alarm.

There are extras like unexpected company, a leaky roof, light bulbs, sickness, a leaky hot-water heater which ruined the linoleum, or going on a trip.

This is not a complete list. A little thought could double it. If you make a list, you will get a visual picture of your routines.

When you marry, your partner may have a list of daily routines that matches yours item for item. Even then, you may differ from one another in the way you carry them out. If so, your two plans for the day will collide.

THE HUSBAND'S FIRST ASSIGNMENT

The process of defining and redefining similarities and differences in handling routines begins before marriage and continues as long as you live.

The husband takes the lead, examining routines that need attention. It is a very long list.

So you begin, two children of God with His love in your hearts—cooperative, committed, submissive. Without His love, your efforts will deadlock again and again.

Does this frighten you? Well, it should jolt you into recognizing that launching and maintaining a marriage is not just a ceremony. You must each carefully study your living patterns.

Blending routines (or becoming one flesh, as the Bible puts it) requires a good deal of study, trial and error, and give and take. It will not be done in a month or even two. You will have many discussions and decisions to face. Get the picture?

Launching a marriage is easy. Keeping it going requires the same time, attention, and effort as a business partnership. And I mean daily effort.

MOVE SLOWLY

Agreeing on how to handle the routines of your marriage boils down to agreeing on policies, procedures, rules, and assignments.

One caution: limit your discussions on particular issues to an hour or less. You cannot handle everything in a day. Some issues may have to wait until next week before you can bring them up. After a while, you will discover that some of your initial procedures and rules are not really satisfactory. They need to be revised.

After a year or two, you no longer deal with first-time decisions. New ones surface continually. Also, old ones need to be changed.

DECISION MAKING REVEALS YOUR SPIRIT

Handling daily routines often produces unexpected surprises. When Eva and I traveled, I usually drove and she watched the map. Sounds good, doesn't it?

I was in for one of those surprises one day when Eva and I were between family life conferences. I had just finished teaching married couples how to get along. I was the expert. All had thanked me for helping them.

En route to the next conference we stopped at a motel. I like to go first class, so we chose the finest motel and slept on the best mattress money could buy.

In the morning, we bathed, applied the appropriate deodorants and perfumes the ads tell us to, ate a good breakfast, and started out in our big, air-conditioned Olds 98.

When you are clean, properly scented, well-fed, well-dressed, in a big new car, and surrounded by gorgeous scenery, you should have it made. All went well until we came to two intersecting freeways. One led to Detroit. The other to Chicago. My intention was to turn on to the freeway headed for Detroit. Eva, the navigator, piped up.

"Henry, you turned the wrong way."

Instantly, I was furious and shouted at her, "Eva, for goodness sake, do you not think I know where Detroit is? I grew up in this state! Do you want to drive this car?"

Having your wife put you down like that is enough to make anyone mad. Mind you, all she was doing was acting as the navigator, doing her job. (Handling routines reveals your spirit.)

I accelerated angrily and glared at the road ahead. Eva did not say a word. Silence filled the car as we sped along.

Then we came to a highway sign by an exit. There was an arrow pointing in the direction we were going. And above the arrow, it said "Chicago."

I am a Ph.D. I am skilled at evaluating data and making accurate judgments from it. Yet I completely ignored that sign and away we went. We came to another exit sign. It said the same thing. I found myself becoming more angry at Eva.

Can you believe it? Notice the limitations of education, good housing, cleanliness, and money. In spite of all these, in a fit of temper, I was acting like a stupid fool.

Still, I decided to try one more sign. Eva did not say a thing, nor did she comment when we came to the next sign, which again said "Chicago." This was the third exit down the pike. We were headed west—not east. I knew that.

Yet my mind was working as fast as it could go, trying to figure out how to get to Detroit without turning around.

How do you get turned around when you are wrong and know it, yet will not admit it? At that moment, you could not have dragged me off that freeway.

There is a way. The Bible says,

> **If we confess our sins, He is faithful and just to forgive us *our* sins and to cleanse us from all unrighteousness.**
> 1 JOHN 1:9

Sounds easy. What were my sins? I have asked this question of many audiences, and their response is so immediate and complete that at times I have had to cut them off.

Pride, rebellion, anger, stubbornness—these are just a few they suggest. It is easy to identify our sins if we want to.

I did not want to face the truth. It was a struggle.

Finally, I told God I was sorry. Would He forgive me? Would He renew His love in my heart? Of course He would. My attitude changed immediately. I told Eva, "I think I am headed in the wrong direction."

I began looking eagerly for the next exit so we could get going toward Detroit.

DECISIONS CAN WAIT

If this stubborn spirit emerges in your discussion, drop the matter until you or your partner repents. It may take thirty seconds, a day, or a month. Whenever, talk to God as His child. He will forgive and bathe your heart with His love. Then get on with the business of settling issues and handling never-ending routines.

A LIFE-CHANGING CONCEPT

Your serenity, peace, joy, and love are not determined by your partner's choices. Your inner condition is revealed, not created, by your partner's choices. Routines will reveal your spirit. Whether or not you let God bathe your heart with His love is your choice. Your partner cannot hinder you no matter how nasty or inconsiderate he or she is.

START WITH FAITH

God's love will help you effectively handle the routines of married life. Remember, marriage involves dealing with a multitude of details on a daily basis.

It takes faith to entrust the deadlocks to your husband's or your wife's judgment. It takes faith from both partners for the husband to make decisions in the best interests of the family, especially when the wife is convinced her judgment should prevail.

Can we say it too many times? Only God's love in both partners will make harmony possible as you handle the routines.

SEXUAL RELATIONS

Everyone enjoys looking at and touching the human body. Advertisers know a sensuous woman or man will catch our eye and our emotions.

Remember your dating days? A thrilling response to your date was as automatic as responding to the aroma of good food or fine perfume. You had no serious problem figuring out how to touch, hug, caress, or kiss. Your problem was restraining yourself.

Is it not strange, then, that so many married people struggle with sexual relations, when touching, caressing, kissing, and intimate relations are the most ecstatic experiences in life—enjoyed by both men and women?

THE MOST COMMON TROUBLE SPOT: SEXUAL RELATIONS

Almost every married couple who comes to my consulting room presents their sex life as a major problem. But never is this the only issue.

A beautiful, shapely lady came, bruised and battered by her husband. They had these slugfests frequently. She usually started them with angry tirades because he came home late or wrote checks without telling her.

When there was no conflict, they had a beautiful sex life. Attitudes toward sex, technique, frequency, or position were not issues. When there was conflict, fist fights replaced tenderness and sexual activity.

This couple illustrates the fallacy that sexual satisfaction enables two people to get along better.

We have all read books and articles that blame present sexual difficulties on parents, early teachings about sex, early experiences with sex, lack of knowledge about how the body is made or about positions and techniques. Not so. People who want to respond sexually will find a way. Information is easily available if it is needed or wanted.

Consider a baby. What determines whether a baby is cuddled, kissed, spoken to with endearing words—or ignored, spanked, and yelled at? In either case, it is the same baby. Yet the parent's response depends on whether the baby is laughing or crying, is digesting its food or throwing it up, has a clean or dirty diaper, is behaving or misbehaving. Then, too, it depends on whether the parent is patient or impatient, angry or happy, self-seeking or serving.

Is your response to your partner the same as to a baby? What is simpler than touching your partner, caressing, kissing, or speaking endearing words? What causes you to pull away, stiffen up, resist? Surely it is not a question of enjoyment. Everyone enjoys some kind of physical contact.

What determines whether you caress or slap? Speak tenderly or harshly? The same beautiful bodies are involved.

The biblical standard for expressing yourselves sexually is total freedom and equality between husband and wife.

Let the husband render to his wife the affection
due her, and likewise also the wife to her husband.
The wife does not have authority over her own
body, but the husband *does*. And likewise the husband does not have authority over his own body,
but the wife *does*. Do not deprive one another
except with consent for a time, that you may give
yourselves to fasting and prayer; and come
together again so that Satan does not tempt you
because of your lack of self-control.

1 CORINTHIANS 7:3–5

In other words, your partner's wish is your command. Wow! You did
not expect such freedom in marriage. Right?

KNOW YOUR PARTNER

General information about what men and women are like will not
serve you here. You must know your partner's needs, likes, and dislikes
to find a mutually agreeable way to express your sexual wishes. It is
God's love in your heart that will serve you, love that
- does not behave rudely;
- does not seek its own;
- is not provoked;
- does not rejoice in iniquity.

The big three become important here:
1. Cooperation
2. Commitment
3. Submission

If the Bible clearly describes total sexual freedom and equality
between husband and wife, what is it, then, that determines whether you
turn your faces or backs to each other?

SELF-SEEKING

As I have listened to people talk about the struggle with their physical response to one another, self-seeking usually comes up as a problem. There are deadlocks over money, housing, social life, church life, family life, in-laws, use of time, or most anything. It is not surprising that they would be deadlocked over meeting each other's sexual wishes.

ACTS OF THE SINFUL NATURE

Also, there are acts of the sinful nature. Unresolved issues between partners reveal reactions of anger, hatred, bitterness, and rebellion. With such reactions, sacrificing sexual satisfaction seems more desirable than pleasing a partner.

By now, you know how to handle the sinful nature. This is a personal matter between you and God. Repent, ask God to cleanse you, and once more bathe your heart in His love.

What if your partner does not repent? Or cooperate? You do not deprive your partner. There is a warning contained in God's Word.

> **Do not deprive one another except with consent for a time, that you may give yourselves to fasting and prayer; and come together again so that Satan does not tempt you because of your lack of self-control.**
> 1 CORINTHIANS 7:5

The only reason for depriving your partner is to devote yourselves to a long period of prayer and fasting. Otherwise, if you deprive one another, you can be tempted seriously.

THERE'S SOMEONE ELSE . . .

"I am married and am attracted to another person to whom I am not married." This is a comment I hear with increasing frequency coming from both men and women, Christian and non-Christian.

I have had individuals who cannot stand the sight of their married partner—much less respond physically—describe a torrid physical affair with someone else (sometimes even a stranger) who is not nearly as attractive or personable as the marriage partner. The new involvement is simply an expression of resentment or retaliation. Surely it is not an expression of the love of God. Physical response is obviously not the problem. It is a matter of the spirit, a matter of the will, not the body.

Granted, there are temptations everywhere. When have there not been? After all, half the people in the world are women, roughly speaking. The other half of the people are men. When you become a wife, all the men out there do not disappear, nor do the women disappear when a man gets married. They are there and are still interesting and attractive.

Beautiful women and virile men were God's idea, you know. You can enjoy the beauty and fellowship of both sexes without lusting after them. You can have many close friends of both sexes. Granted, these relationships are sometimes hard to handle.

A MATTER OF COMMITMENT

Marriage involves commitment to one person, even though other people are still there.

A child of God, with the love of God in one's heart, who means to cooperate with one's partner, who means to submit, and who proves it in other areas, will not have a sex problem with one's partner. Note the conditions. Take the Bible seriously and you will be on your way to a beautiful sex life. You will want to please your partner.

What if your partner gives you a cold shoulder in spite of your willingness to follow the biblical command? Stay available. Desire to do your part. Remember, these problems are not solved in a day or even in a year. Your commitment is to God. Your commitment does not depend on your partner's choice. You stand by, yielding to the love of God. He will sustain you. Love endures. That is good news, not bad news. Try it.

MONEY PROBLEMS

Yes, sex is the struggle people discuss the most in the consulting room. But in strong second place is the struggle of money. I have had to help hundreds of my clients work their way out of financial trouble.

Here is my homespun advice.

No one has trouble spending money. The challenge is how to keep some of it. Anyone who has some money has obviously not spent all of it. People in financial trouble have spent more than they have made. Sound elementary? Yes. But to ignore this simple fact is to get into trouble.

Where do you begin if you are in trouble? First, draw up a financial statement of your assets and liabilities. If you do not understand what I mean, then seek out someone to help you. Now you must face your creditors.

Second, if bill collectors are hounding you, go to each person to whom you owe money and frankly discuss your situation. Then work out a payback agreement with him. You may need to turn to someone who has experience in handling money. This may be a humiliating experience, but again, you may need some counsel.

The important step is the will to do it. This may mean some drastic changes in your lifestyle.

MY STORY

Let me share with you a bit of my own story about finances.

I will be eternally grateful to an inexperienced Christian education director and a Sunday school teacher for their help.

First, the Christian education director. He was always asking me what I was doing with my money. I figured it was none of his business. But he kept it up anyway. He kept rubbing my nose in two Bible verses:

> **"But seek first the kingdom of God and His right-
> eousness, and all these things shall be added to
> you. Therefore do not worry about tomorrow, for**

**tomorrow will worry about its own things.
Sufficient for the day *is* its own trouble."**
MATTHEW 6:33–34

After months of trying to push these words of Jesus out of my mind and avoiding that minister, I finally gave in. I got out a pencil and sketched out the use of my time and money.

After I did my work, looked after the yard, played tennis, went sailing, my week was up. I spent very little time at home. All my money was spent on me and mine. My life was the reverse of what Jesus taught in those verses.

I promised Jesus I would obey His commandment to seek first His kingdom. This was a new way of life. Gradually, I developed a new set of priorities. Here they are:

1. Wife
2. Children
3. Ministry
4. Making a living

Such priorities required a drastic change in my lifestyle. My emphasis changed from money, money, money to thinking about my family and service to people. This emphasis drew me into the church and eventually into changing from engineering to counseling and teaching. This gradual change began when I was twenty-seven and continues to this day.

We developed a new financial plan also. Whatever income came along, big or small, we divided it as follows:

- Tithe   10%
- Living expenses/savings   85%
- Risk money   5%

I could not imagine how I could give away 10 percent of my income as a tithe, but we decided to do it. This has been one of the best financial decisions I have ever made.

THE RISK MONEY WAS THE KEY

Why five percent for risk money? The idea was planted in my mind by a beloved Sunday school teacher, a very wealthy man. I was working on my Ph.D. at Cornell University at the time. I decided to study full time, so I asked this man to lend me the money to do it. He did, but added a little speech:

"Henry, I am lending you this money to show you I believe in you and to encourage you. This is like lending you one of my finest tools. This is part of my 'risk money.' You see, I use money to make money. When I lend it to you, I cannot use it. I am investing in you."

Wow! I heard this speech and made two commitments as a result:

1. I would see to it that this investment in me paid off.
2. I would also build up some risk money.

So that is how rich people do it. If you want to have money, you cannot spend it all. I vowed to set aside 5 percent of my income as investment money like the rich people.

This fund accumulated slowly at first, but I kept looking for an investment. Across the years, the Lord has given me wisdom far beyond myself for handling that money. Starting from zero, that money has been multiplied hundreds of times and has made it possible for me to give many thousands of dollars back to the Lord's work.

I will spare you the details but leave you with the principle once more: if you tithe and put aside some risk money (assuming you seek first His kingdom and righteousness), God gives you the wisdom to multiply it.

How do I know? Because I have been privileged to help many people straighten out their tangled financial affairs, to establish priorities, and get on their feet spiritually and financially.

You and your partner must determine your percentages between you and the Lord. There are books in any library that will counsel you as to your financial problems. Many banks and lending institutions also provide materials on handling money.

As I said at the beginning, this book is not a detailed financial guide.

My purpose is to challenge you to learn how to multiply your money to the glory of our Lord and get your priorities in order.

FACING CHANGE: A COMMON PROBLEM

One of the toughest adjustments a marriage faces is sudden change. There are job changes or losses. There are moves, unexpected pregnancies, sicknesses, broken bones, financial reverses, financial gains. The children grow up through various stages. They leave to launch their own careers. How well you meet the changes depends on how committed you are to your God and your partner.

FOR THREE YEARS . . . THE POORHOUSE!

Calvin and Liz were broke all the time because Cal was going to medical school. He barely had time for any part-time jobs, and Liz worked full time teaching third grade at an elementary school near their mobile home.

There was never any money left over. It all went for school expenses and the minuscule budget they had set up.

But they were happy. They were dedicated to one goal: getting Cal that title of Medical Doctor. Liz took her hard schedule without complaint. Cal helped whenever he could and made sure he kept his grades up. Together, they reached their goal.

They literally had been in the poorhouse, just the basics in food and seldom any new clothes. Somehow, they enjoyed it.

Cal joined two other doctors in a successful private practice. In a year, Cal became a full partner. Only twelve months away from poverty, Cal and Liz were approaching prosperity.

Calvin's job fascinated him. He worked long, hard, satisfying hours. Soon, they had retired their past debts. Now, he and Liz became fascinated with gadgets, boats and trailers, clubs, cottages, specialty foods, expensive restaurants, entertainment, and whole wardrobes of new clothes.

Their social life turned them on as well. Cal headed up a cancer drive for a year. Liz was pushed to the head of the women's group. She was consumed with her new interest in the tennis club as well. Calvin was ape over golf.

Only a few years ago, they had been living in poverty. Now Cal and Liz were completely caught up in these new, pleasant, challenging, fascinating experiences. By now, a child was born and being raised by baby-sitters.

Gradually, it began to dawn on Cal and Liz that they were unhappy. They did not see much of each other anymore. When they were together, there was more bickering than fellowship. The whole thing was confusing. Where did the teamwork and fellowship go that was so precious to them while Cal was in medical school and Liz was helping him through?

Now they were going separate but interesting ways. The marriage was suffering. They were playing singles again. So they ended up in the consulting room. How could two brilliant, educated, talented people with ample money to spend end up like this? It seemed they had the world at their feet.

This is a garden-variety kind of problem, like the common cold. It is ageless. It was happening back in the apostle Paul's day. He wrote,

> **I know how to be abased, and I know how to
> abound. Everywhere and in all things I have
> learned both to be full and to be hungry, both to
> abound and to suffer need.**
> PHILIPPIANS 4:12

Cal and Liz had not learned this secret. He was trained in the medical profession but did not know how to handle prosperity.

Multitudes of Americans like Cal and Liz have not learned how to handle prosperity. Their prosperity brought out clearly in them the drive to go your own way. Prosperity revealed a lack of love of God. They learned that education, brilliance, and wealth are not substitutes for God's love.

WHAT WAS THE ANSWER?

Cal and Liz—intelligent, talented, prosperous—needed a Savior. Through Jesus they could let the love of God bathe their hearts. They needed to submit themselves to each other. Cal needed to take leadership in the home. He needed to look after his relationship to his wife as he did to his own body.

This was a stiff dose for Cal and Liz. They fought these steps for many months before realizing they could not do it on their own.

YOU CAN COUNT ON CHANGE

Changes will occur. No one orders his own life to come out as he wants it to. It was Jesus who said:

> **"These things I have spoken to you, that in Me
> you may have peace. In the world you will have
> tribulation; but be of good cheer, I have overcome
> the world."**
> JOHN 16:33

Read what the apostle Paul wrote:

> **And we know that all things work together for
> good to those who love God, to those who are the
> called according to *His* purpose.**
> ROMANS 8:28

IT WILL BE GOOD

Is your partner going back to school to enter a profession? Is there sickness? Unexpected pregnancy? Poorly handled prosperity?

How could these circumstances work together for good? But they have. No one understands the benefits of trials, difficulties, or conflicts as he goes through them. But for a child of God, with His love in your heart, it all adds up for good. As you look back, you see the benefit. As you go through the day or peer out into the future, you trust God.

The child of God has a zest for life. So bring on the future! It will be good. With God as your source, you can expect to respond to life as the apostle Paul describes it:

> **Rejoice always, pray without ceasing, in every-**
> **thing give thanks; for this is the will of God in**
> **Christ Jesus for you.**
> 1 THESSALONIANS 5:16–18

CHAPTER 11

Meeting Inevitable
Changes

And we know that all things work together for
good to those who love God, to those who are the
called according to *His* purpose.
ROMANS 8:28

God will unravel seemingly insurmountable problems and solve a
seemingly hopeless situation when there is submission to Him.

In this suspense-filled world of ours with its dramatic changes, one
fact is certain—the certainty of uncertainty. You can expect the unexpected to happen. The mature person, especially the Christian,
approaches the changes of life with interest, enjoying the variety and
meeting the challenge.

One of the great tasks facing marriage partners is that of accepting
the fact of change. In a marriage there is a continual series of changing
events which demand a constant adjustment of both husband and wife.
Pregnancy, the arrival of each child, the absence of children, moving,
neighborhood changes, church responsibilities to assume or to give up,
the shifting scene at school—these are some of the changes that come to
each couple, with their corresponding adjustments.

At times husbands or wives say their partner is not the person they married. Of course not. Just as your children keep changing as they grow up, so do you. At age one, your children act one way; at two, another way; at three, still another way; at five, differently again. A married person certainly cannot complain about lack of variety. There is a continuous change.

We must remember, however, that a marriage sometimes will develop in one way when we want it to go in another way. At such times there may be periods of disorganization when one solution is attempted, and then another, over a period of weeks or months. The chapters in a marriage are often unexpected and unpredictable. To expect an unchanging partner or unchanging circumstances, to expect to live happily ever after automatically as in the fairy tales, is not true for this life. To expect a permanent point of perfect adjustment and happiness is unrealistic. There is no family on earth that has had this experience.

Continuous change is the normal experience in any marriage. This means that there must be continuous adjustment. This can be done with tenderness and compassion if you realize that the family is not a static organization. Marriage must be worked at. It doesn't just tick along in perpetual, unhindered motion. Satisfactory adjustment requires proper and free communication. It means sharing joys, giving praise, and taking admonition or correction. It means we must strive for complete understanding among all the members of the family. This is not an easy way. However, it is a workable way and leads to a peaceful, joyful life together.

When the unexpected happens to you, just remember that this is no exception. This is normal. Your peace and happiness depend on your relationship to God. His peace is available during uncertain, unexpected times as well as during certain, stable times. You are not alone. The Father is with you. Unity and agreement must be maintained. Paul says to us:

**I, therefore, the prisoner of the Lord, beseech you
to have a walk worthy of the calling with which**

you were called, with all lowliness and gentleness,
with longsuffering, bearing with one another in
love, endeavoring to keep the unity of the Spirit in
the bond of peace.
EPHESIANS 4:1–3

Dedication to this goal is only the beginning. A husband and a wife
have a lifelong task ahead of them. A business needs constant attention
to keep it running smoothly. A tennis team must practice constantly in
order to win the game. A marriage, too, needs constant attention in order
to preserve unity and agreement because changes occur inevitably in any
marriage.

ALL THINGS WORK TOGETHER . . . FOR GOOD

Ken had been offered a college teaching job even before obtaining his
bachelor's degree. This enabled him to get started in graduate school and
set up a lovely apartment. Alice, his wife, became pregnant, so they happily looked forward to starting their family. The future looked good.

Some of the other men on the faculty were worried about getting
drafted because they had never served in the armed forces. Ken had no
such worry because he had been in the Navy during World War II. One
day a letter came from the Navy notifying him that he was recalled to
active duty. He was to be given an immediate overseas assignment in a
remote corner of the world.

An unexpected, irreversible change had come. His wife pregnant, a
career interrupted, advanced education put aside, his home disrupted.
And none of the other faculty men were called.

In a matter of weeks Ken was whisked away, leaving Alice to figure
out what to do with herself for two years. She tried keeping the apartment. Then she went to live with a friend. Finally, she decided to join her
husband overseas. Why did this happen to them? What would this do to
his education and career?

I think of the promise:

And we know that all things work together for
good to those who love God, to those who are the
called according to *His* purpose.
ROMANS 8:28

This verse seemed farfetched to Ken and Alice and to those who looked on. Ten years have passed. Ken's second stint in the Navy can be viewed in the perspective of time. It turned out to be a good thing. They learned how much they appreciated one another and that they could, when necessary, live apart. They learned that seemingly insurmountable problems can be solved, that a seemingly hopeless situation will eventually unravel. Ken has his Ph.D. degree, the kind of job he wanted, a son—and an extra maturing experience thrown in.

Why did it happen? Only God knows. But He promises,

For I know the thoughts that I think toward you,
says the LORD, thoughts of peace and not of evil,
to give you a future and a hope.
JEREMIAH 29:11

In his booklet, *Tragedy or Triumph,* Dr. Donald Grey Barnhouse tells of visits to two men, each sick with tuberculosis. The first one became very angry and began to curse. "Why does God make me spit my lungs into this cup? God is so cruel to me!" He cursed God for his suffering.

The second man had to spend twenty-three hours each day in bed and could be up for only one hour. One night he spent his hour walking and stopped in to rest where Barnhouse was preaching. He heard the story of the love of Christ and received Jesus Christ as his Savior and Lord. From that time on, he used his daily hour to witness in the neighborhood. Soon he was too weak to go out. He asked Barnhouse to come to his home to preach to his friends. They were seated upstairs on the kitchen floor. After the message, this sick man said, "I know that the next time you are all together it will be for my funeral, and I want to witness to you about Christ." A few days later he died, triumphant in Christ.

Barnhouse goes on to explain:

> I believe that God permits whatever happens to an unbeliever also to happen to a Christian. The unbeliever cries out against God, but the Christian says, "Lord, do to me whatever You please." No matter what your condition in life, if you are not a believer in Jesus Christ, God has a double of you somewhere who is believing in Jesus Christ. If you are in the Home for Incurables, and do not know Christ and think your lot is terrible, someone else in the Home for Incurables is praising God. The devil has his doctors, and God has His doctors who live in simple faith and trust the Lord. The devil has his lawyers who connive and cheat; God has His honorable, upright lawyers who seek to aid those in difficulty. God has His rich men and the devil has his.
>
> Describe yourself to me. Tell me how old you are, what is your education, what are your circumstances. I will duplicate them in the life of some Christian. To put it the other way around, whatever happens to a Christian, the same is happening to an unbeliever, and he is crying out, "God, you can't do this to me!" but the Christian can say, "O, God, You can do anything You wish to me. You redeemed me. You bought me with Your blood. I am Yours, and I know that all things will work together for good because I love You."

TESTED BY FIRE

Peter reassures us:

> Beloved, do not think it strange concerning the
> fiery trial which is to try you, as though some
> strange thing happened to you.
> 1 PETER 4:12

He says again

> that the genuineness of your faith, *being* much
> more precious than gold that perishes, though it is
> tested by fire, may be found to praise, honor, and
> glory at the revelation of Jesus Christ.
> 1 PETER 1:7

Change tests the mettle of the Christian. Change comes frequently to every family.

Some families have learned to anticipate change and to live with it. Others are fearful of what tomorrow may bring, and their uneasiness has them so unnerved that when change comes they are floored. Still others refuse to recognize the inevitability of change, and through an unnatural striving they seek to ignore it, to go on their way as if nothing had happened.

Think of the changes in family life since 1900. The labor-saving appliances born of electricity have revolutionized housekeeping. The automobile has moved us away from the streetcar track and into suburbia and even beyond to exurbia. Two world wars, a major depression, and mounting inflation have stimulated changes in morals, customs, outlook, residence, and spending. These can be called universal changes. For the most part, they have been gradual, almost creeping.

On a more personal note, families are touched by changes that affect them but not necessarily their neighbors or townspeople. A baby is born. A second one comes bringing situations that were not known with the first one. A youngster enters school, a father is given church responsibilities that require much of his time. A teenage son asks to use the family car for the first time.

Change came to John Simpson when it looked as if the road ahead ran straight to financial success. He owned a gas station on the edge of a large city. It had taken years to build up his business. When offered $750,000 for the business, he could turn it down with honest casualness. Then on another day, after returning from lunch, Simpson walked into the station to meet a man waiting to talk with him.

A new state highway, the man told him, was on the drawing boards. It would come right past Simpson's corner—and clip off his gas station in the process.

He would be paid according to a fair appraisal of the property. Another piece of land might even be offered in trade. But the work of years would be gone. He would no longer be on one of the best corners. He faced years of an uphill fight all over again.

John Simpson and his family experienced a change that hit deeply. So did Mike Sisco when the auto plant he had worked in for thirty-two years closed. He was too old to get another job that amounted to much. He and his wife adjusted to the change as well as they could. They would live more simply and make their clothes and other possessions last longer. But within three weeks the neighbors, perhaps unaware of the changes that had already struck the Siscos, petitioned to have their street paved. The hard-pressed Siscos faced a payment of $2,500 that threw their new austerity budget off-kilter.

In a brief period the following changes were entered on one person's prayer card file for just three families:

> Harry Thomases—Harry quitting job for another necessitates family moving to neighboring state. Letter tells of their attending church. They now describe it as evangelical, not like one they attended here. All members of family accept Christ as Savior.
>
> Robert and Evelyn Brown—Longtime leaders in the church, both teaching Sunday school, singing in choir,

faithful at prayer meeting, active in calling program. Evelyn very sick, must drop out of everything. Don't see much of Robert anymore. Has had to give up all but his job to care for Evelyn and the three small children.

Jack Wilsons—Jack has better job now. Family longs for TV. Bought it and can never pull away from it even for Sunday night church.

SUDDEN OR UNEXPECTED

Change may bring a severe test of the family's inner strengths. At such a time, how well a family has integrated its values and beliefs into its day-to-day living will be demonstrated in its ability to cope with the change.

What particular change provides the family's greatest testing? Only you can say for your family as you undergo change. Remember, gradual and expected changes may have just as great an effect over a long period as sudden and unexpected changes. Let us look briefly at both types.

DEATH

No change is as heart-searching as death. It causes even the most hardened to pause and examine himself. One of our children's class-mates, a junior in high school, was killed in an automobile accident. A man and his wife in our church were returning home from shopping. He slumped over the wheel and was dead at age fifty-five. Another man, a pillar in his church, went to the doctor complaining of the flu. He died of a heart condition in the doctor's office.

Death is to be expected. It can be sudden and without warning. It will be the day-by-day faith, the values and goals which direct your life, that will come into play when you are confronted with the death of someone dear to you.

Surely the death of the father is a change that strikes a family from many directions. Cast on the wife is the burden of keeping the family together and providing a living for herself and the children. Her task will be greatly eased if they have anticipated the possibility of such a change and have planned for the continued existence of the family after his death. Life insurance is an almost universally accepted resource to hold the family together after the father's death. But preparations other than economic ought also to be made. Some may be as commonplace as teaching the wife and the older children do-it-yourself jobs that usually wait on Dad's doing them.

But if money is available, most household or family business services can be purchased. What cannot be bought is the influence of a father or mother on both the remaining partner and the children to help the family continue and successfully meet its challenges, even after the valued member has been taken by death.

Many are the examples of a mother's or father's prayer life and wise discipline guiding the children for years after the parent has died. Many have proved the promise in James 1:5:

> **If any of you lacks wisdom, let him ask of God,**
> **who gives to all liberally and without reproach,**
> **and it will be given to him.**
> JAMES 1:5

The death of a parent has proved to many a remaining parent that God will give you wisdom to act alone. It is God who is most important in your life.

In some instances, death may not be the change that tugs the hardest at the family's ability to adjust. Look at some other common changes.

SICKNESS

Long-term illness of one member of the family will bring out whether the other members possess the spiritual fruit mentioned by Paul:

But the fruit of the Spirit is love, joy, peace,
longsuffering, kindness, goodness, faithfulness,
gentleness, self-control. Against such there is no law.
GALATIANS 5:22–23

An automobile accident put a child of the Jackson family into the
hospital. For months, the family made a daily trip to the hospital to visit
the child. Without such visits, which were happy times for the little
patient, restoration of health might never have come. A drastic change in
the family schedule was necessary, and it was not always easy for the
family to make the trip or to be at the bedside the minute visiting hours
began, but they did it cheerfully. Patience enabled them to adjust to the
change.

A family accepted the change sickness brought. The mother was frequently ill and finally the doctor sent her to bed, ordering her not to get
up as long as the disease persisted. No one desired that the mother be
shut off in a bedroom away from the mainstream of family life. So her
bed was moved to the living room. A bed in the living room? This family was willing to make a change that others, because of pride, would
have found impossible.

SEPARATION

A new job in another city can bring about temporary separation. So
can the frequent traveling of a father in his work. Permanent separation
comes when marital conflict has led to a breakup of the home.
Temporary separations may cause some new roles to be adopted or old
ones shed for awhile with the willingness to go back to the former status
when the separation is over. The loss of a parent from the home—
through death, legal separation, or divorce—means some roles must be
altered permanently and may involve not only the remaining parent but
the children as well.

ECONOMIC

A pay raise can bring about change as can a reduction in income, or even loss of a job. Economic change can be up or down, gradual or sudden. The values a family holds will be important in their reaction to such change. If they live on a materialistic plane, sudden wealth can ensnare them in a ridiculous display. Their inability to handle money wisely will be readily seen by their friends and neighbors.

The Bible gives sound advice on reacting to economic change. Paul tells how he learned to live with the extremities of being abased and abounding and how, regardless of his state of affairs, to be content (Phil. 4:11–12).

Bill Mays never had much of this world's goods until he married Ruth. He then sought the help of his mother-in-law, which she generously gave. But he despised her as a person. When he was abased, he thought to abound would be happiness. When he abounded, he was not able to handle himself any better. He could not see God's hand in his mother-in-law's handout.

Job changes can mean a shift in hours, upsetting established routines. Changes at the office or shop can bring a promotion that wins accolades. Or they may result in a passing over for promotion or a demotion that prompts raised eyebrows and thinly veiled curiosity.

Economic change may mean Mother going to work, forcing her to take on the role of breadwinner and to decide how she is going to apportion her time among family, church, and community.

ENVIRONMENT

Better or poorer housing may be in the future for your family. Or for some other reason a move to another neighborhood may be necessary. A change in neighborhoods means a change in neighbors, possibly in the school the children attend, the family church, in long-established habits of shopping or getting to work or to music lessons. Moving day usually is the prelude to numerous new experiences that seriously affect family life.

In an America in which environmental change seems to be the key to the day—reflecting a population explosion, the march of decadence in our cities, and counteracting urban-renewal programs—neighborhood changes can come to the family that stays put.

The cornfield-to-carport trend has put many a farm family into the heart of an urban situation. In neighborhood shifts, thousands of families have had to face up to racial issues. As the makeup of communities change, the vague feelings on hitherto distant and impersonal problems become specific feelings. Theories must be translated into actions. As a family is swept into the changing city or mushrooming suburb, complex pressures threaten the stability of the home. More than ever, the Christian family will be driven to cling to its unchanging foundation.

THREE UNCHANGING PRINCIPLES

Change should never be a surprise. You need not look on it as something wrong. Even creation will undergo cataclysmic changes.

> Of old You laid the foundation of the earth,
> And the heavens *are* the work of Your hands.
> They will perish, but You will endure;
> Yes, all of them will grow old like a garment;
> Like a cloak You will change them,
> And they will be changed.
> PSALM 102:25–26

> All the host of heaven shall be dissolved,
> And the heavens shall be rolled up like a scroll;
> All their host shall fall down
> As the leaf falls from the vine,
> And as *fruit* falling from a fig tree.
> ISAIAH 34:4

The state of the believer also is to be changed. Paul wrote to the Corinthian Christians that

> we shall be changed. For this corruptible must put
> on incorruption, and this mortal *must* put on
> immortality.
> 1 CORINTHIANS 15:52B–53

But in the midst of change, we can be sure of three unchanging principles. They go back to the foundation on which the Christian home is built.

First, God does not change. The psalmist says of him:

> But You *are* the same,
> And Your years will have no end.
> PSALM 102:27

Malachi quotes the Lord as saying,
> **"I do not change."**
> MALACHI 3:6

James speaks of the
> **Father of lights, with whom there is no variation**
> **or shadow of turning.**
> JAMES 1:17

The writer to the Hebrews says,
> **Jesus Christ *is* the same yesterday, today, and forever.**
> HEBREWS 13:8

Second, God's Word does not change. Hebrews 6:17 (NIV) speaks of the "unchanging nature of his purpose." The psalmist says:

The counsel of the LORD stands forever,
The plans of His heart to all generations.
PSALM 33:11

Forever, O LORD,
Your word is settled in heaven.
PSALM 119:89

Third, the state of the believer will change, but not his standing before God. In his treatise on what changes and what does not, the psalmist says of the believer:

The children of Your servants will continue,
And their descendants will be established before You.
PSALM 102:28

The Christian, therefore, is able to look on changing circumstances through eyes that see an unchanging God. He is able to order his life according to the unchanging Word of God. He can do this and know that his future is secure because his relationship to God can never be disturbed by the forces of change.

If this is in the foundation of the Christian family, the shocks of change can be withstood, even though they reach to the very footings.

You will experience changes that call for adapting to them, but the Christian family must adapt to change within the framework of its values and beliefs. We are reminded again of what Jesus said about foundations. One house was built on a rock, the other on sand. Violent weather changes came. The house on the solid foundation stood, the other fell.

Some changes we pursue, hoping they will bring a better, more pleasant, perhaps more fruitful life. Some changes we become aware of as we grow older. This you find out when, as parents of growing children, you try to keep up with them, only to discover you are not as young as you once were.

In many instances, however, it is not man's nature to desire change. Rather, we tend to be fearful of the unknown and would rather become moss-covered in our old ways than risk the new. But life cannot be lived only according to what has been. Life is change. Wise is the admonishment to "get on with the living."

So, as you live with your marriage partner, try it God's way. His way is not only the best way for the Christian but is the "only way" for the Christian. You will find that God's way brings fulfillment and happiness with an abundance of life!

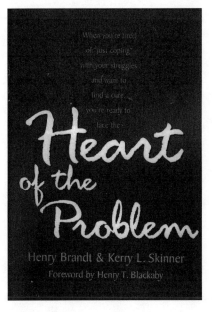
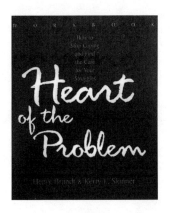